All Holidays 2020
First Annual

AN NCPA ANTHOLOGY

A Collection of Fiction and Nonfiction Holiday Stories by NCPA Authors and Poets

Barbara Klide, Jackie Alcalde Marr, Sharon S Darrow, Amy Rogers, Norma Jean Thornton, M.L. Hamilton, Frances Kakugawa, Vicki Ward, Scott Charles, Charlene Johnson, Judith Vaughan, Susan Beth Furst, Laura Roberts, Denise Lee Branco, Bob Irelan, Elaine Faber, Steve Pastis, Bobbie Fite, Christine "Chrissi" L. Villa, Linda Villatore, A.K. Buckroth, Emma Clasberry, Barbara Young, Sandra D. Simmer, Ronald Javor, RoseMary Covington Morgan, Kimberly A. Edwards, Roberta Davis, Barbara Barrett

ALL HOLIDAYS 2020: First Annual

A collection of fiction and nonfiction holiday stories by NCPA writers and poets.

Published by
Samati Press
P.O. Box 214673
Sacramento, CA 95821
www.sharonsdarrow.com

This book is independently published by Samati Press in arrangement with individual members of Northern California Publishers & Authors: www.norcalpa.org.

Printed in the United States of America

ISBN: (paperback) 978-1-949125-21-4
       (ebook) 978-1-949125-22-1

LCCN: 2021900232

Table of Contents

A CHRISTMAS COFFEE CRUISE

BARBARA KLIDE

We were on Christmas holiday. During a previous holiday our goal was to search for the best in European chocolate, influenced by a long-ago tour of Hershey's Pennsylvania factory where awestruck kids, including me, watched vats of chocolate being stirred. We would later find our prize, a delicious bar of dark chocolate and hazelnuts called *Kitin*, once produced in Spain, but now long gone

Our new holiday adventure was about coffee—A Christmas Coffee Cruise.

My first introduction to coffee was at a time when few had heard of specialty brands. Most only knew the big names like *Chase & Sanborn, Hills Brothers, Maxwell House, Folger's* and *Chock-Full O' Nuts*. I'd smell the intoxicating percolated coffee of one of them wafting through our little NYC apartment one evening each month when it was Mom's turn to host a game of Mahjong. There she would serve coffee along with a plate of large hand-broken chunks of refrigerated chocolate from a smooth one-pound Hershey's bar. Each morning, I would smell the milder *Sanka*, "97% caffeine free" made with fine, powdery grinds that she would spoon out of a glass jar. A product, originally from Germany, it took off in France where the name Sanka literally means "sans caffeine".

As a young woman, I would later be found custom-grinding and selling beans behind a raised counter at *In the Beginning Natural Foods*, a little shop I had opened in San Francisco. There we sold imported chocolate bars, bulk herbs, vitamins, fresh produce, natural food cookbooks, raw *Alta Dena* dairy products (until pasteurization was enforced), and soy milk, a unique new product to the American market at the time. Being a small-time purveyor of coffee, the store only sold Italian, French Roast, Colombian, Brazilian and Ethiopian Arabica beans.

Coming full circle, my companion and I now embarked on a multi-city Christmas cruise on the fabled Rhine River named by the Celts— "raging flood", flowing from the Swiss Alps to the North Sea.

Our first shipboard meal was a formal affair with Christmas music playing in a dining room bedecked with holiday decor. I regrettably arrived five minutes late inviting such a stern reproval by our German hostess that I seated myself at the table five minutes early every night thereafter, hands folded in my lap.

Dinner was served on heavy stoneware plates and was prepared with a medieval feel about it including deeply savory meat, potatoes and vegetables. The feast should have been an impossible feat to follow, but then the coffee arrived. As to pronouncing its acidity, aroma, body, and flavor as a professional coffee connoisseur might do, as an amateur, I could only describe it as shockingly dark and as stern as my scolding. In spite of smarting from the humbling I'd received, I could do nothing but admit that this German coffee was the most perfect brew I'd had up to that time and that my conventional American tastes would forever be changed.

Cruising on the river, we saw many fairytale-like castles and fortresses; a few crumbling and others turned into restaurants and hotels. We also passed through multiple locks which are part of a waterway system allowing vessels to navigate through uneven depths. For some, including myself, the castles and locks began to blend into one another after every turn of the river no matter how intriguing they all were.

When we arrived at each ancient city, we would admire the museums, the architecture, cathedrals, and those castles available for touring. They were all adorned for Christmas making them warm and inviting. We sought out the cafes and quickly realized that our host country revered coffee. It was prepared black or with condensed milk in brownish salt-glazed stoneware mugs keeping it hot. It was mostly drip-brewed using filters likely because *Melitta*, a familiar brand in the U.S., was invented in Germany.

After days on the river, we came to appreciate the convenience of cruising from city to city with our luggage left safely on board while we trekked through each new port and returned to our own cabin at the end of the day. All told, the cruise was captivating and we were impressed with the coffee we experienced, with the shipboard coffee getting our top prize—for the moment.

We planned to leave the cruise before reaching Amsterdam to enjoy an extended stay in Paris. Up until now, the farther north we went, the stronger the coffee tasted. Then we arrived in Paris—the center of the universe for coffee and pastries. The French managed to turn coffee into an art during the 350 years since it had been introduced to them.

Our initial cup of French coffee checked off every box, and so did the pastries. This was at a time when café noir was café noir, meaning without milk or cream because it was perfectly delicate and dark, needing nothing else. Whether one took it with a lump of raw sugar, a splash of cream, or neither, this Parisienne coffee was velvety fine with an aroma that practically had us in a trance. The cup of divinity was served in our own hotel in pure bone white porcelain cups and saucers. Surrounded by Christmas flourishes—everything was perfect. We had refills and I must confess we were each guilty of having two insanely decadent chocolate croissants to go with it.

In this state of oblivion, we dodged a tragedy that might have caused us injury or worse from a terrorist bombing at the museum's train station where we were supposed to be that morning. It seems a spate of attacks had been taking place, but by grace and gluttony we were saved.

The French Gendarmes began to well up everywhere and especially at the tourist attractions. Their weapons were locked and loaded and outright fear of more bombings convinced us to leave Paris early and continue to our final stop—Amsterdam.

Before we took off, we squeezed in visits to several

cafés and particularly loved that dogs, some with holiday ribbons on their leashes and a few wearing Christmas sweaters, were present at the feet of their humans.

Between that first flawless German coffee and the nearly spiritual experience of its Parisienne counterpart, we agreed the latter was our favorite.

We settled on taking a train to the Netherlands to enjoy the countryside, but French train workers had just begun a train strike that crippled our plans, leaving us no choice but to book a flight instead. Fortunately, the airlines were free of worker disputes.

On the bus to the airport with neither of us reading nor speaking much French, except for our new go-to phrase, "*café et chocolat croissant s'il vous plaît*", we mistakenly hopped on a local rather than an express bus to *Charles De Gaulle Airport.* When we realized our error, we'd missed the flight, and sought an overnight airport hotel room—a pod, really, that made my companion, Monsieur 6' 4" as it were, appear to have taken Alice's Wonderland pills that make you large.

The next morning, we found ourselves at our airport terminal greeted by a stunning 25-foot image of Michael Jordan at the top of an escalator, but at the gate the greeting was not so fine. An official-sounding, but nervous voice came over a loud speaker and a friendly Parisienne traveler translated for us when we appeared confused by the escalating chatter around us. It seems unattended luggage had been discovered at our very gate and airport security protocol required that it be blown up—but of course.

This was pre-September 11 where the entire terminal would have been placed on lockdown. We immediately noticed people closer to the boarding doors putting their fingers in their ears and so began what could only be described as the "wave" that might be experienced at a sports stadium. Instead of having fun standing, waving our arms and sitting back down in succession, we put our fingers in our ears in a wave that extended from one end of the packed gate to the other.

Luckily, we did not miss our flight again because the

authorities quickly pronounced the situation in check. The explosion, loud and jolting, took place as we were warned, but clean-up efforts never happened. We made our way through the gate watching the sun streaming through the tall windows exposing the motion of all the lint debris lazily circling around in every direction from the blown-up luggage. On the ground was a lone sneaker and other ordinary traveling items that oddly escaped disintegration. It occurred to us that to hold off cleaning might have been a pre-determined plan to get people boarded without delay, which it did. They could tidy up later.

We finally arrived in Amsterdam to a magical Christmas holiday with a dusting of snow, decorations everywhere including the brightly lit canals, and joyously-singing street musicians. After a good night's sleep, we were pleased that our hotel provided complimentary coffee, the darkest, heaviest coffee; rough around the edges. I am being kind. It was straight up battery acid, but thick, and smelled and tasted like you ran out of coffee and dug yesterday's coffee filter, grinds and all, out of the smelly trash and brewed it up again. I could feel my eyes widen, my face scrunching up, and my body slowly going into shock. The coffee did no justice to the distinction the Dutch had earned by delivering the word "*koffie*", later to become "coffee" into the English language in the late 1500s.

Either way, we just knew we could do better, so we headed to a *koffiehuis*, not to be confused with the famed Amsterdam coffeeshops for buying and smoking cannabis. We were rewarded with a heavy brew that was more refined, quite flavorful and as dark as ever to go with the great food offered in this city, one of the international centers of Europe offering ethnic cuisine from all corners of the globe.

On our last evening before the next day's flight back to the U.S., we were cruising around on foot and found ourselves staring down a brick-paved street. We had wandered into what is known as the Red-Light district. It has the notoriety of persons legally selling themselves from behind plate-glassed window shops that were dressed up like one might find at Macy's around this time of year. The only difference was that the red neon lighting in these windows was decidedly less Christmas and more "suggestive" than the sparkling Yuletide green, gold and red lights that we saw all over Amsterdam.

Now this is a self-directed coffee holiday, but hey, we were in Amsterdam and decided to stroll down the street and experience "window shopping" for ourselves. Unlike department stores, no window decorators would change out these "mannequins". These were the real deal who walked in and out of the display on their own power.

We stopped in front of one window decorated with a lady resting on a comfy-looking chaise lounge with a silhouette that stood out—I'm talking about the chaise. It was curvaceous and could easily make a perfect statement piece in your own home with tufting, turned wooden feet and glamour to spare. The lady poised on it seemed merely to be accent décor for the furniture with a matching bolster pillow tucked under her arm comfortably propping her up.

We noted she was reading a book as if she were on a break. Staring a little longer than we should have, her eyes suddenly looked up. In liquid motion she eased herself off the chaise to the window and smiled large. We were embarrassed voyeurs on a short detour from our innocent coffee journey.

She took us completely off guard when she pointed her long-painted fingernail in our direction with an unmistakable, full-on come-hither move to which my companion pointed to himself and mouthed, "Me?" *Silly boy,* she seemed to say shaking her head, and with an even bigger smile, pointed to me.

I'd never heard such a bawdy laugh come out of my pal's barrel chest, but it broke the awkwardness of the moment. At that point I grabbed him by the elbow and tugged him in the direction of our next destination, to get one last Dutch-brewed coffee.

Without thinking, I found myself looking back. Instantly I thought that I would turn into a pillar of salt. As if to confirm that notion, I found her with her hands on her hips flashing me one last smile.

We savored our cups of coffee served in charming porcelain blue and white coffee cups that somehow made it taste even better. We laughed a lot, chatting about this last shop's beautiful Christmas atmosphere while sipping a hot cup of the darkest steaming brew of our trip. We could only describe it as heady, full-bodied, and well, distinctive in a sort of "kinky" way—the coffee experts might object, but it just seemed to fit.

After a long flight back across the Atlantic, we landed at *O'Hare International Airport* and crawling through the concourse, followed the most iconic logo in corporate history—the two-tailed mermaid. The Siren, hovering above the heads of travelers, was luring us on. Like two poor souls dying of thirst in the desert, we followed her to *Starbucks'* oasis where we met others like ourselves and settled in at the end of an exceedingly long line.

Finally, at the counter we ordered a pair of leaded Grande Caffè Mochas, desperately needing to power up for the next leg of our flight home to California. The syrupy-sweet coffee did not disappoint—it proved itself to be life-giving.

Leaning up against a wall, we admired the simple charm of *Starbucks'* Christmas-red paper cups. Not lost on us was that through her green window, the Siren was staring back at us with a vaguely familiar smile.

Happy that we were getting closer to home and that our hands were nicely warmed up holding the hot containers, we toasted to a joy-filled and "Merry Christmas."

Born in NYC, Barbara Klide is author of *Along Came Ryan…the Little Gosling King Trilogy*, the true saga of a mated pair of elegant, sensitive and smart Canada geese and their offspring that nested three years in a row where Barbara works. She donates book profits to various wildlife rescue groups.

Barbara graduated with an MBA from Golden Gate University, San Francisco, and a Certificate in Graphic Design from the University of California, Davis. She is Director of Marketing for Quest Technology Management, California and a member of NCPA. She also has a story in four other NCPA anthologies.

Her Canada goose compendium series has received much acclaim including from Dr. Lorin Lindner, PhD, *Wolves and Warriors*, as seen on Animal Planet and Bill Bianco, President, Audubon Society, Sacramento.

Barbara and her longtime partner reside in Fair Oaks, California where they rescue, foster, and adopt-out cats. Visit Barbara at: Barbaraklide.com.

THE GIFT

JACKIE ALCALDE MARR

It had been several years since I'd seen Kris. Even so, I still loved him, and I knew he still loved me. Ours was a love that would last forever. So, I was anxious to see him, but I waited patiently.

The holidays were such a wonderful time at Margaret and Carlo's home. I loved being there every year as they got into the spirit. The trimming of the tree was always a treat, with the leisurely recounting of stories as the kids reached for their favorite ornaments. This year, 2002, promised to be the same. As always, Margaret sat me down across the room so I could be out of the chaos. I caught a glimpse of myself in the mirror and realized my pearls surely needed to be shined up, but Margaret didn't seem to notice at all. Or maybe she was just being polite.

"There you go, my dear," she said as she put a steaming cup of tea on the table beside me and flashed me a loving smile. She was such a caregiver. I swear she never stopped moving, always wanting to make everyone else comfortable. Sometimes I think she accommodated too much. Even Carlo saw it.

Oh sure, he soaked up her doting, but even he would eventually say, "That's enough, Babe. Sit down and relax."

Margaret and Carlo were always so in love, and it showed in more ways than one. I suppose the most obvious was the fact that they had four children, all in a row. Caroline was the oldest, then John, Ryan, and the youngest, Julie, arrived two years after Ryan. Margaret handled it all gracefully. She just buzzed around those kids, making sure everyone had whatever they needed. You can imagine what Christmas was like each year, the base of that tree crammed with packages of all shapes and sizes, and the children eager to wake up on Christmas morning to create piles of torn paper and mountains of toys.

I sat in my chair, as always, watching the familiar scene as they placed hooks on each ornament, found a space on the green tree, and stood back to admire their work. This year Margaret seemed unsettled, a little nervous somehow. She kept shuffling the boxes of ornaments, and at one point she muttered, "I'm not sure we should do this."

Caroline shot back, a bit impatient, "We've gone over this, Mom. This year we're doing Christmas here, just like we used to. The kids are looking forward to it."

Oh my, how Caroline had grown! I can still remember when she was the only toddler in the house. Well, they were all adults now with children of their own. And those children would soon have children too. It was so good to see how they'd all turned out. Margaret and Carlo did a fine job with them, and just look at the wonderful family they'd made.

I watched as John and Ryan pulled the train cars out of their boxes and assembled them on the track that meandered around the base of the tree. "You can barely see the Lionel logo anymore," John said with a little melancholy in his voice.

"A little paint is all it needs," replied Ryan. "This set is in great shape. Shoot, these trains are collector's items now."

Christmas Eve was the main event that we all looked forward to each year. "Open house" would begin around four o'clock and often lasted until two in the morning. A constant stream of friends and family would come through the door, and the house would swell with so much laughter, music, and chatter that I imagined a fairy tale view of the windows bowing out and the house throbbing with joy in the cold night air. The lights on that tree would blink, sending shards of color bouncing off the curled ribbon that adorned all those packages. The kids and their cousins would run through the house, screeching and playing their own games, dodging around the legs of women dressed in their finest and men with high-ball glasses jiggling with ice and twists of lemon. Then we'd hear the thunder of their feet as that herd of children ran down the stairs to the basement, their private lair where last year's toys lived.

Margaret would be in the kitchen, a gaggle of women surrounding her as she readied another plate of cookies or made a fresh pot of coffee. Carlo was usually manning the fry kettle on the spare card table, placing an endless stream of fragrant linguica sausage into the pan and breaking open a sourdough roll to serve up the next guest.

I would hear him bellowing, "C'mon, we have so much. It's not picante. Amaral's is the best, you're gonna love it!" A soft haze would drift from the kitchen into the living room, heavy with the scents of smoked paprika, cinnamon, *Chanel #5*, and of course, Uncle Tony's pipe.

The old stone fireplace was constantly aglow, crackling and sending an occasional pop of orange ember through the black chain mesh screen and onto the hearth. The hi-fi stereo would play through endless Christmas albums, pausing only long enough for the next record to drop and the needle to find its first groove.

The kids' favorite was *Little Drummer Boy*, but I was always partial to *Holly Jolly Christmas*. Of course, Kris liked them all, but I think he liked *Silent Night* the best. Carlo loved the crooners – Bing Crosby, Nat King Cole, Dean Martin – but no one could compare to Frank Sinatra. Carlo played those albums the most. When Sinatra sang *Let It Snow*, Carlo would usually find Margaret wherever she was, and they would dance. Oh, how they would dance! They twirled and shuffled, coming apart but never losing each other's hands, then spinning together as though they were merged into one heart and soul. It was so effortless and so beautiful!

Of course, that was forty years ago. I know people just don't do this like they used to when those kids were growing up. Getting gussied up, traveling to reconnect with loved ones and catching up on the details of their lives. I do get a little sentimental about that era. Everyone had a nickname, like "Pogie" and "Dee." And everyone knew each other – *really* knew each other, firsthand. The Christmas Eve event was sacred. It's a shame, really. Those grandchildren just won't experience the holiday in the same way. But I still appreciated the tradition of it all and the people who came every year.

Speaking of which, there was still no sign of Kris, but I knew he'd show. I waited patiently. And where was Carlo? He must have been barbequing out back. He usually had some venison from his fall hunting trip, and he loved grilling it up when the kids came for dinner and decorating.

Caroline hung an angel on the tree, its wings sparkled gold, and it wore a black graduation cap. As her daughter Annie reached up to hang a bell on a high branch, Caroline pointed to her angel and said with pride, "Your grandma gave this to me when I graduated from junior high." She paused as Annie examined the ornament in the glow of the red light that lit the branch beside it. Then Caroline continued, shaking her head, "Gosh, that was so long ago."

It's amazing how the years twist and turn, bringing new adventures and tragedies, all unforeseen until the next bend in the track. I'd seen them collect so many memories over the years.

"What about this one, Mom?" Annie asked as she held up a ballerina with a fluffy silver tutu.

Caroline took the ornament from her furtively and placed it back in the box, whispering, "That was Aunt Julie's – the year she won the dance recital. Let's put it away, it will make your grandma sad."

I saw it, but thankfully, Margaret was rummaging through a box and didn't notice their conversation. It was true; it would make Margaret so sad. Julie had lost her battle with breast cancer when she was only forty-two years old. Christmas really wasn't the same after that. It was like the big hole in the Christmas tree that you just can't hide with lights or ornaments. Although it's still a beautiful tree, the hole is there, gaping, and everyone still sees it.

Uh oh, Margaret gave up on that box and came around to see what Annie and Caroline were doing! Annie hastily snatched another ornament from a box and thrust it into Margaret's hand, "Tell me the story of this one, Grandma." It was an innocuous looking ornament, a monkey wearing a Santa hat with a bugle at his lips. But Annie knew that each of the ornaments had a story and her grandmother loved to tell them all.

"Oh, goodness," Margaret said. "This was the year your uncle Ryan learned to play the trumpet, and your grandfather and I thought we'd go mad." Annie giggled, and Ryan looked up from the train set.

"Hey, I loved playing the trumpet," Ryan said as he connected another rail car on the track.

"Yeah, you loved it a little too much," Margaret said. "Your father and I were so glad we could send you to the basement to practice, but that sound came straight up through the heater vents. It was like you were playing right here in the living room."

Everyone laughed, and Margaret reached up to hang the little monkey on a branch. I was shocked to see her hand shaking violently, and Caroline took the ornament from her. "Let me help you, Mom." Margaret pursed her lips, annoyed. But she let Caroline take the ornament, and she came to sit in the chair beside me.

When had she become so frail?

She touched my hand lightly and just smiled at me. I smiled back; thankful I could give her a little comfort. But she didn't sit long. In a moment she was back up, dragging a little stool toward the tree and opening the next boxes, hanging each ornament with great care.

"There you are!" Margaret exclaimed as she stood up. And there he was, across the room. Finally! My heart was so full I was afraid it might crack open. He looked the same as ever. Well, maybe just a little older. After all, we all get older, right? But he was certainly aging well. I hoped he'd feel the same about me. His eyes twinkled a bit as he came along beside me, and my hand slid into his, just like it always had. It felt so right - him in his chair and me in mine, side by side again.

"Tell us the story of that one, Grandma," Annie pleaded.

"Well," Margaret started, sitting in the chair next to us again. "It was December 1945, and the war had just ended. Everyone was so happy. Your grandfather had been stationed in France, and he was finally coming home." She paused for a moment, "You kids are so lucky you haven't

13

lived through a world war – such a terrible thing." Her voice trailed off as she closed her eyes and shook her head slowly.

"We know, Mom," said Ryan. "Go on with the story."

She opened her eyes, smiled at me and Kris again, and then her tears welled up. As she blinked, one rolled down her cheek and fell to her blouse, leaving a dark spot on an otherwise sky-blue chest. She put the little wooden sign gently in her lap and pulled a wadded-up *Kleenex* from the end of her sleeve to dab her eyes and nose. Usually when she told this story she was cheerful. What was going on this time? The kids all waited silently, allowing her to regain her composure.

She continued, "He had to wait in Paris. It took some time, you know. There were so many men coming home, and they had to give over all their gear and wait for their transports. He always told me that those were the longest days of the war, waiting in Paris, waiting to come home to me." She dabbed her eyes once more, the *Kleenex* fluttering in her shaky hand.

"The city was still in shock, but people were already trying to reclaim their lives in whatever way they could. He and a few of his buddies went to a market one day, and he came upon a booth where the family carved Christmas figurines. He said they were beautiful. There were several carved reindeer with sleighs, holly wreathes, glittering trees and stoic wisemen. Then he saw this pair with their jolly red suits, their warm smiles, and their tiny sign. As soon as he saw them, he said, he knew he had to bring them home." She closed her eyes and put her hand to her heart before continuing.

"And we were lucky he made it home for Christmas. So many men had to wait months more for their turn. But he made it. It was the best Christmas ever that year." She looked into my eyes and then into Kris' eyes. She plucked the tiny wooden sign from her lap and placed it at our feet where it belonged. Like every year, she read it out loud when she set it into place, "Our love is the gift that lasts forever." Her gaze landed on our hands, perfectly nested

14

together. "He loved these figurines – Santa and his wife, sitting in their matching chairs, holding hands. They've been with us all this time." Another tear rolled down her cheek. She sat in the chair beside us again and said in a soft and sorrowful voice, "I can't believe he's been gone nine years. I still can't believe it."

So that was it. Carlo had passed away. That's why it had been so long since we'd been together, Kris and I. Nine years. No wonder she was so sad. My heart just broke for her. I wished I could make her feel better. I wished I could tell her that it would be OK – that she and Carlo would be together again someday. Look at me and Kris. Just like them, we'd seen year after year of life and love in this home. And then we were suddenly separated. Even though we were kept from each other for years, tucked away in our dark boxes, we were reunited in the end. She and Carlo would be too, someday. Time has a way of bringing us back together.

And just like our little sign says, their love will last forever. I know it. Kris knows it. Carlo knew it when he bought us in that Parisian market, brought us to his home, and placed us on this table. And in her heart, Margaret knows it too.

Jackie loves wine, nourishing old friendships, all things Spain, and the lessons of history. She is a lifelong learner and loves to pack her bag for adventure.

After a long corporate career as an organization development leader, Jackie became an independent consultant, trainer and certified leadership/life coach. She created Evolutions Consulting Group to help individuals and groups achieve their goals while accentuating their core passions. She works with private, public, and non-profit organizations, as well as individuals who are creating fulfilling lives.

Jackie co-authored *Social Media At Work: How Networking Tools Propel Organizational Performance* (Jossey-Bass).She has been published in the Sacramento Business magazine, the Organization Development Journal, and NCPA's Travel Anthologies.

She's currently writing the story of her family's immigration from Spain through Hawaii to California and a memoir for her young granddaughter. She lives in Folsom with her husband Jeff and their mischievous mutt, Quincy Noodlebutt.

ANYTHING HALLOWEEN
NORMA JEAN THORNTON

It's Halloween, the "funnest" time of the year
When kids dress up, and it's OK to spread fear

A scarecrow, a pumpkin, a silly monkey
Even the *Thing* ~ he's so big, strong and hunky

A spider, a skeleton … a spooky bat
A princess who's wearing some fairy tale hat

A talking skull, a witch riding a broom
A new vampire bride and her ghoulish groom

A green Ninja turtle, who'll keep all from harm
From the zombie ahead, and his voodoo charm

A goblin, a ghost, a witch with a cat
Nothing unusual 'bout any of that

Frankenstein, staggering, with screws in his neck
He looks a little old … but … oh, what the heck?!

A little red devil with horns and forked tail
There'll be one each year, it never will fail

Raggedy Ann & Andy, Superman, a spooky rat
While a slimy witches' brew stews in a black bubbling vat

Lights off, it's dark ~ I wait, in costume, by the door
They'll get all their treats ~ plus a little bit more

Spooky music, moans and groans
Whirling winds and rattling bones

Suddenly, a howl … and a scarier sound
Little ones run screaming, around and around

Anxiously we wait for Halloween to get here
Both young and old love it, and enjoy it each year

HANUKKAH PAPER

SHARON S DARROW

Our daughters went to bed late on Christmas Eve, right after Stan told them he heard sleigh bells in the distance. That did it. They ran straight upstairs, determined to fall asleep fast so Santa wouldn't pass up the house. Everyone knows that if kids are still awake when Santa lands on the roof, he flies away and may not come back.

"Thank goodness, I thought they'd never go to sleep," Stan said. He'd checked on them to make sure they weren't still talking and giggling under the covers.

"No kidding." I walked into his arms for a hug and quick kiss. "Help me get the stuff out so we can get started."

From the first Christmas with our oldest child, we'd created a tradition of wrapping all the gifts together on Christmas Eve. We'd play music on the stereo, light a big fire in the fireplace, and stack all the bags and boxes we'd hidden around the house and garage into the living room. We always went overboard on Christmas for the sheer joy of shopping together, and then the fun of watching the kids' faces when they opened each gift. My space was in the center of the chaos, with tubes of wrapping paper, tape, name tags, ribbons and scissors stacked near me. Stan would wrap too, but his primary job consisted of supervising the process and placement of each finished present in just the right spot under the tree. Well, they started out under the tree, but ended up filling the whole end of the room.

After an hour or so, it was clear we had a major problem. "Honey," I said. "We don't have enough paper. In fact, we've got less than half of what we need."

"How did you manage that?" Typical man, the shortage had to be my fault.

"I don't know," I replied, well aware of how to avoid an

argument. "But no matter, we have to have more wrapping paper."

"On Christmas Eve? Nothing is open tonight!" This was the early 1970s, when most stores and businesses were closed on Sundays and almost nothing stayed open on Christmas Eve.

"You'll have to find paper somewhere."

"Can't we use something else?" Stan looked around the room, then stood and checked the kitchen. "Maybe newspapers or aluminum foil, or something."

"Or what? We don't have much newspaper, not even close to enough. Forget about foil, we're talking about wrapping gifts, not a turkey. And there isn't anything else."

Grumbling under his breath, Stan grabbed his coat and keys. "I'll see you when I see you."

Wrapping wasn't as much fun alone. I plodded on until I'd used up all the paper—leaving a very large stack of gifts waiting to be wrapped. Where in the heck was Stan? It'd been over two hours. I was beginning to get worried. Not about him, but if he didn't hurry, we'd never get all the packages wrapped in time. Things were tougher back then with no GPS units, no cell phones, and no Siri to call up for the nearest open store or gas station.

It was almost another hour before Stan stumbled in the door, looking both triumphant and grim at the same time. He'd driven all over town, from one all-night gas station to another, checking out their racks of holiday goodies. At long last he found one lonely station over ten miles away with a half-full rack of paper rolls. Stan grabbed every single tube and hotfooted it out of there.

"Here." He thrust the rolls at me. "I've done my part. Now it's your turn." He plopped down on the couch and stretched out.

I was so thankful for the paper that I didn't care. I was surprised not to see any red or green patterns, just pretty blue, gray, and gold. Oh well, the kids wouldn't notice. I grabbed my first package and got started. Odd, I'd never noticed wrapping paper with gold geometric patterns before, but it looked really pretty on the present.

The next roll was even more interesting. The background was light blue, but there were funny wooden things with odd strange figures on the sides. Oh well, too many boxes to wrap to worry.

When I reached for the third roll and saw candelabrum, I yanked out the last two rolls and looked closer. Sure enough, one had little squares with tops, candlesticks, and Jewish stars, while the last one just had writing—Happy Hanukkah!

"Stan," I yelled, waking him from a nap in front of the television. "You bought Hanukkah paper for Christmas presents."

"Huh?" More asleep than awake, he was not getting the message

"You bought Hanukkah paper for the kids' Christmas gifts. And I've already used up a lot of the paper, so you can't even take it back." That last phrase got him up. Up and straight to my side.

"I don't care what's on that paper, it's not going back." He knelt down and looked at the unopened tubes. "That is the only paper I found in this entire town. I wouldn't care if it had dancing alligators or leprechauns on it, you have to use it."

"How can I use it? Our girls expect presents wrapped with Christmas pictures, you know, Santa or snowmen or Christmas trees. What are they going to think?"

"They'll think it comes off just as fast as the other kind. All they'll look for is the nametag."

I disagreed, but had no choice. Hanukkah paper it was. As I wrapped, I was running scripts through my mind on how to explain the meaning of Hanukkah to two little girls. I knew what menorahs were, but how in the heck could I explain about dreidels? I'd heard about the wooden tops, but had no idea of their significance. And if one of them asked about why Hanukkah was celebrated with eight days of giving instead of just one, I could just imagine the mercenary gleam in their little eyes. Great, now I'd have to hit the encyclopedias for research before going to bed.

Bed was heaven when we finished the last gift at just

after four in the morning. Naturally, the little monsters who loved sleeping in on other mornings jumped on our bed screaming "Merry Christmas" at six-thirty. Neither threats nor bribery worked on Christmas morning, so we crawled out of the covers and headed downstairs.

The girls oohed and aahed over the transformed living room that Santa had magically filled, then opened their Christmas stockings while Stan fixed his coffee and I made hot chocolate and cinnamon rolls. Only after Stan and I settled down in favorite chairs near the tree did the process begin. Each girl was allowed to find a present with her name on it and start undoing in seconds what had taken me so long to create the night before.

I kept waiting for questions about the unusual wrapping paper, but neither daughter even noticed. Stan was right, they only saw pretty colors and bright ribbons—and, of course, nametags.

That was the last time we ever took a chance on running out of wrapping supplies on our Christmas Eve marathons. We kept up the tradition though, adding more fun to wrapping as the girls got older by adding multiple nested boxes, bricks and rocks for weights, and taping every single edge of paper. We loved the mystery of Santa and added little notes in funny handwriting to all the nametags from Santa and his elves.

Planning was the key, we thought, and were sure we controlled every possible variable on future Christmas mornings. We did too, for just a couple more years. I still remember the morning when our youngest, worn out from unwrapping all her loot, looked around with a thoughtful expression and said. "Wow, Santa brought so many great things. But where are the presents from you guys?"

Sharon S Darrow is an entrepreneur, business owner, award winning author, public speaker, and an expert in caring for neonatal orphan kittens. Two of her books are about animal rescue: *Bottlekatz, A Complete Care Guide for Orphan Kittens* and *Faces of Rescue, Cats, Kittens and Great Danes*. Two are inspirational, a memoir titled *Hindsight to Insight, A Traditional to Metaphysical Memoir* and *Tom Flynn, Medium & Healer*. Her fifth non-fiction is a training manual about publishing, *Navigating the Publishing Maze, Self-Publishing 101*. She also writes historical fiction. *She Survives, Strive and Protect,* and *Desperate Choices* are the first three books in the Laura's Dash series, inspired by her maternal grandmother. Sharon firmly believes that life just gets better and richer, the longer you live. Her personal motto is "Find harmony within, then all things are possible."

Her website is https://www.sharonsdarrow.com, and you can reach her via email at sharon@sharonsdarrow.com.

THE HATCHERY

AMY ROGERS

Her granddaughter-in-law, Luz, didn't want her help in the kitchen. If green bean casserole and sweet potatoes had been on the menu, she would've insisted on picking up a paring knife. But lumpia? She was useless. Seventy-five years ago, when she was a child in Nashville, people fried *chickens*, not rolls of...whatever was in Luz's homemade lumpia. Apparently, Martin, her grandson and Luz's husband, really liked them. So Filipino Thanksgiving it was. As a guest in her grandson's home, she had no right to criticize the holiday meal planning.

Luz breezed past with her long black hair flowing. "Can I get you a glass of tea, Nana?"

"Thank you."

The tea was cold and sweet, but not quite sweet enough and with not quite enough ice cubes. Joe, her husband, knew how to make tea the way she liked it, sometimes with bourbon. She didn't suppose this household of almond milk drinkers had any bourbon.

She lifted her mask to sip the tea. When she failed to immediately pull the fabric back over her face, Luz gave her a worried look.

I'm not going to wear this thing all day. What was the point? She shared a home and a bed with Joe until his fever topped a hundred and one. By then, she must've been thoroughly exposed to the coronavirus. Besides, everybody has to die of something.

She'd been thinking that a lot since Joe's funeral, when they wouldn't let other people come mourn with her.

The front door opened. "Nana!"

Gabriel, her five-year-old great-grandson, exploded into the house. He barreled into her knees. Iced tea splashed over her fingers and dribbled to her lap.

His father trailed behind at grownup speed. "Slow down, tiger," he scolded.

"He's alright." She broke the COVID rules and wrapped her arms around the boy. Virtual school, hardly any friends to play with—what was he supposed to do with all that energy?

"*Lávese las manos*," Martin said. Gabriel wriggled away from her and dashed to the bathroom.

Joe had picked up some German while serving in West Berlin after the war, but she had never learned a word in a foreign language. This was America. Why would she? Only in recent years it seemed like she was hearing accents and non-English conversations more and more. Now even in her own family. Joe disapproved. She wasn't sure.

Gabriel burst out of the bathroom, hands dripping. "What are you doing, Mama?"

Luz held aloft two mixing spoons while she leaned over to elbow-hug her boy. "Mama's busy right now. Go play your game."

She knew that didn't mean jacks or checkers. It was electronic games. Hours and hours in front of screens. The digital babysitter, and now school too. Why didn't they send him outside? He could make his own games.

"You doing okay, Nana?" Martin asked. "Can I get you something?"

His tone oozed concern. She clenched the glass. He meant well. They all meant well.

But resentment and anger burned in her belly. She hated this new role. She hated the pandemic, the helplessness, the restraint, the sacrifices. The loss—no, she would not think about the loss.

Instantly she made up her mind. "May I take Gabriel to the fish hatchery?"

Luz was crouching in the kitchen, her head in a cabinet of pots and pans. "That would be great."

Gabriel's widening eyes focused on her.

"You want to go with Nana to see some fish?" the father asked.

The boy jumped up and down. "YES!"

She smiled under her mask. Fish and dinosaurs, dinosaurs and fish, were her great-grandson's obsessions.

"I can call you an Uber, Nana," Martin said.

She would rather walk the four miles than deal with that. "No, I can drive us. There won't be any traffic today."

Martin helped Gabriel into his car seat. Even strapped in, the boy was in constant motion of limbs and head. While she drove east of the Sacramento suburban home, Gabriel talked nonstop.

"Did you know T-rex had these little tiny arms? And triceratops had three horns?"

"Hmmm. Are you excited to see the fish?"

"Nana, you know you're not supposed to eat the salmon right now?"

Joe had been a fisherman. Never the fly-fishing kind, just old-fashioned bait and tackle. They'd saved up and taken a cruise to Alaska once. Joe fished for salmon with a guide. They shipped the frozen meat home. She cooked it for him with butter and brown sugar. He loved it, talked about that fish for years after.

"Why can't you eat them?" she asked.

"Well you can, but they're spawning. Spawning means they don't taste good."

She chuckled. "I see."

Brilliant sunshine fell on the parking lot at the Nimbus Fish Hatchery, rapidly raising the temperature of the late morning air. A perfect Thanksgiving Day in California. She heard the roar of water from the American River canyon just to their right, and smelled dead fish on the breeze.

"C'mon!" Gabriel ran ahead, knowing exactly where the action was.

She followed, musing about how many decades had passed since she last visited the hatchery. She used to bring kids here—her kids, other people's kids. She used to have a purpose.

"Nana!" he shouted.

"Hold on."

She chose her steps carefully. A fall on the cracked pavement would certainly ruin everyone's day. Gabriel pushed into a cluster of people gathered at the sloping concrete wall ahead. They moved away. She put on her face mask. She couldn't understand why the mask over her nose and mouth seemed to dampen the noise of the falling water.

Gabriel was just tall enough to lean over the wall. He yelled and pointed.

Clear, cold water tumbled from one level to the next in the fish ladder. They named it wrong, she thought. It's a staircase, not a ladder. At each rung, or step, enormous fish swam in a small pool. Most pointed their noses straight into the current, swimming fast enough to hold their place. Then every twenty seconds or so, one of them would leap. The breathtaking effort was incredible to see. Sometimes they would make it, their sleek, exhausted bodies sailing through the air and landing on the next level. Sometimes the water and the height pushed them back, and they plunged into the starting pool. Either way, the salmon would stop fighting for a bit, then swim right back into the flow.

That was life, wasn't it. One endless struggle against an unwavering current. Every year around Thanksgiving, the salmon came here to spawn, and die. Death was the reward of their ferocious, body-sapping effort.

Gabriel sprinted back and forth beside the fish ladder, too excited to stand and watch only one step. A fish splashed him. He squealed with delight.

The spawning run was nature's way, but it looked so stupid. The fish crowded, pushed, drove blindly upstream. Did they know what they were in for? A dam blocked their natural spawning grounds. The world had changed, but they had not. At the top rung of this ladder was a slaughterhouse.

She had to look away.

"Come on, Nana!" Gabriel grabbed her hand and pulled her toward the egg-harvesting facility. "This is where they get the eggs!"

Because it was a holiday, the facility was quiet. Tomorrow the conveyor belt would carry unconscious, stunned salmon. She knew from previous visits that workers would separate the males from the females. Males would be "milked" for sperm. Spherical orange salmon eggs, unnatural in their perfection, would spill out of the bellies of the females and be collected in tubs. The bodies would be tossed aside for rendering into fish meal.

Gabriel stayed at the fish ladder for about fifteen minutes—something like an eternity for him. Then he insisted that they go to the raceway ponds.

The white noise of the water faded as they walked away from the stream. Gabriel struggled to decipher the latch on a chain link fence door. She opened it for him and they stepped into partial shade under a vast stretch of netting that protected the ponds from sun and birds.

The raceway ponds were like the fish ladder but flat and much, much longer. Moving water in row upon row of these long, narrow tanks shimmered and rippled. Gabriel took off down the aisles at a run.

She peered into the water. Salmon. Thousands and thousands of salmon. But not like the decrepit, desperate spawning fish in the ladder. These were fingerlings, young salmon just a few inches long. Vigor and energy seemed to radiate from the water as the fish swirled and sparkled. Like Gabriel, they were in constant motion.

"Nana!"

He was back and standing at a vending machine, turning the knob round, trying to collect a few pellets left behind by the last paying customer. She found a quarter in her purse.

"Put your hands under the spout. Like this." She made a cup with her hands.

Gabriel's hands filled with fish food. Ecstatic, he ran to the nearest pond and threw it into the water in too-large clumps. The young salmon responded with a frenzy, splashing, vacuuming up the food at rocket speed.

All the struggle, all the sacrifice of the previous generation led to this, a teeming pool of eager new life.

She put another quarter in the machine and gave Gabriel most of the pellets. She kept a few for herself. They smelled fishy and left a greasy film on her skin, the final oily remains of the ones who made it to the top. She dropped the pellets one or two at a time into the water.

27

Her great-grandson laughed and threw them recklessly, without restraint.

With pure joy.

Her heart swelled with love.

For everything there is a season, and a time for every purpose under heaven.

A time to plant, and a time to harvest.

A time to be born, and a time to die.

She had so much to be thankful for.

*Eccclesiastes 3: 1-2

 Amy Rogers, MD, PhD, is a Harvard-educated scientist, professor, award-winning author, and critic who switched from teaching university biology classes to reviewing, writing, and publishing science-themed thriller fiction. Her novels *Reversion*, *The Han Agent*, and *Petroplague* use real science and medicine to create plausible, frightening scenarios in the style of Michael Crichton. Compelling characters and fictionalized science—not science fiction—make her books page-turners that seamlessly blend reality and imagination.

Amy lives in Northern California where she also runs ScienceThrillers.com and is treasurer for Northern CA Publishers and Authors. Her nonfiction articles about science and engineering behind the scenes of everyday life first appeared in the *Inside Arden* newspaper and are now collected in her book *Science in the Neighborhood*. During the pandemic crisis of 2020, she became a trusted source of accurate, accessible science information through her blog at AmyRogers.com.

Visit her website to learn more. Amy@AmyRogers.com
Facebook.com/ScienceThrillers

THANKSGIVING PROMISE
SANDRA D. SIMMER

Be thankful for your blessings
Whether they are great or small,
For valuing God's precious gifts
Brings happiness to all.

Reach out your hands to others,
To share your simple meal.
Kindness and generosity
Helps the world to heal.

Unite the different cultures,
Blend all the colors of mankind.
The creator doesn't make mistakes,
He wants our lives entwined.

God has a purpose to his plan
His children can embrace.
Love conceives communities;
Frees religion, creed and race.

Give thanks that you are living
In a time of strife and pain,
For out of darkness comes the light
To lead us home again.

THE HOLIDAY CONSPIRACY

NORMA JEAN THORNTON

HALLOWEEN
6 Sep 2003

These stores do it to me every time ... and most likely several million other women (possibly even some men - but certainly *not my* husband!).

Just when the weather starts *feeling* different, the air has that special smell and there are rustlings and remnants of past memories from this time of year, the stores take it upon themselves to stock up on all that neat Halloween, Thanksgiving and Christmas decoration stuff – even though it's still only the first week of September 2003, almost two months from the earliest, "*funnest*" (as our younger grandkids would say), and greatest decorating holiday – *Halloween.*

We just went to Walmart to drop off some film to be developed – *only!* Needless to say, I came out of the store with over $100 worth of merchandise, as usual; it's entirely impossible for me to "just go in for one thing" and the conspiracy crowd knows it!

That's why they pile on all those fancy new-fangled gadgets that go round and round, up and down or here and there – singing or playing merrily along, if not chattering and bouncing or dancing and giggling away.

But the piece-de-resistance is the bright colors of everything. Even after more than sixty years, the child in me goes wild and wants it all ... and I have my own money to buy it!

The little villages for Christmas have always fascinated me, therefore I have three or four ... also one for Halloween, and each year they become more elegant and detailed. Today the store was in the process of setting up a fabulous

Halloween scene, and had there been a price anywhere, it most likely would have been mine, even though it's quite large and I have no idea where we could even put it.

But that's never stopped me before! We'll just have to make a place if we can't find one; somewhere in between the two trains we don't have room for and all that other miscellaneous moving, singing Christmas things – oops, forgot we're talking about Halloween –

So instead, somewhere between the moving wailing witches and goblins ... wild fiberoptic trees and black cats or spiders ... and that other Halloween village there's already no room for. Oh well ... where there's a will, there's a way - and if I wind up buying it, I *will* find that *way!*

ADDENDUM 31 Oct 2020:

I did find that way ... along with many more ways, for many more Halloween fun things ... as well as Christmas things.

Not quite two months short of seventeen years since I had written the above from a 2003 shopping incident, everything is the same, with the exception that I'm many years more than sixty-something, now being just two months shy of eighty.

AND there are at least seventeen more of those even newer-new-fangled widgets and gadgets, for both Halloween and Christmas sitting around the house, inside and out, as well as in one of the three sheds, purchased for just such things ... and more.

Matter of fact, just three weeks ago during my now monthly, instead of weekly thanks to Covid-19, trips to Walmart, since it was obvious there wouldn't be much need for Halloween candy, again thanks to the Corona pandemic, I only grabbed a couple of bags of the candy my grands and great-grandkids like, instead of the normal 10-12 bags of a variety.

My cart looked ... and felt ... empty, and my fancy was once more titillated by all those Holiday things, so I made up for lost shopping-time over the past eight months, by shoving everything that appealed to me into my cart.

Cart piled high and overflowing, and more than $300

later, I had bought every single one of those things that were stacked in it, but this time, instead of keeping all of them myself, I'm using some as Christmas gifts for my local kids, and the huge musical Christmas-song playing battery-operated train with tracks that totally surround a Christmas tree, went to the 3-year-old great-grandson for his October birthday. Good thing I didn't buy more candy, since the only trick-or-treater that came by was that 3-year-old October birthday-boy.

The bonus this time, I don't have to worry about finding a place to put all that fun stuff I bought; this year, instead, my kids can worry about it, since they're getting them as presents!

CHRISTMAS
6 Sep 2003

I don't know what it is, but each time I get in a crafts store like Michaels, or Walmart when it's set-up for a holiday, I become little Miss Susie Home Maker and want to get busy into crafts!

As though there aren't at least (I'm being very honest here, believe me) nine-hundred-and-ninety-nine "crafty" things to do in my crafts room at home already.

I buy things … in multiples … so the grandkids and I can work on them when they come over, but then either forget where I put the things, don't feel like it when they're here, or don't think about it until after they've gone home.

Unfortunately, I go to the store again, and buy more, and more ... and more! ... then *even more*, because the conspirators keep bringing out something new … and fun to do!

At that point, there are so many things stacked around it's impossible to even get in my crafts room until I clean it out again … and once I get things cleaned and *organized* in there, I can never ever, ever, find what I'm looking for again.

I've always been a sucker for Santas and angels, but those merry-go-rounds with that delightful music also reel me in. Especially the ones that actually move up and down and go 'round and 'round. *This* year seems to be the year of

33

the merry-go-rounds; the one I bought today makes number three in the past two months, and they aren't cheap!

This one not only plays authentic merry-go-round music, but also Christmas music – fifteen songs of each, and they all sound great.

Every year I try to buy some new, unusual, special item at Christmas-time and I think this one most likely ties as my favorite, with the Russian angel that hubby bought me in Texas several years ago. The angel's wings move to the Christmas music she plays,

However, there are still several intriguing Christmas doohickeys left, and it's awfully early in the year. So early, it can't even really be considered Christmas season, and besides, this one *does* play non-seasonal, real merry-go-round music too, so can actually be used any day, so who knows? This may be the year for *two* new toys for granny!

* * *

By the way … hubby had no part in what was bought. He was just along for the ride, and to keep me from buying more; too bad he went to the car and left me standing forever in the check-out line right in front of that merry-go-round!

* * *

ADDENDUM 31 Oct 2020:

Yes, it was the year for two new toys, and even though it's now seventeen years later, they're all still here and working, along with the other ones I've bought each year since 2003.

And, since the loss of my husband in December 2005, I've found it hard to take down the Christmas tree each year, because that was always his job, one I never liked to do. He also always set the tree up, and added the lights, for the same reason.

In 2015, a couple of days before Christmas, I got a really good buy on the floor-model already put-together, floor-to-ceiling gorgeous fake tree. Brightly decorated with tiny white blinking lights, the store was just putting it on clearance to get rid of, when I was in line at the register in the nursery department ... where all those fun and tempting things are, naturally ... my favorite registers!

Even though I already had a tree up and decorated, I grabbed this one before anyone else even knew what was happening, and had to stand guard over it until my son got there with his truck to take that huge tree home, help finagle it through my front door, and put it in the house, already set-up, still in one piece, even after the hairy trip through the front door!

The local granddaughter helped decorate it, and it's been standing in the middle of the living room floor ever since, lights on, 24/7.

It made a great night-light, until unfortunately, those lights just recently burned out, so I'll have to mess with working around all of the ornaments to drape lights around the tree the day after Thanksgiving, this year. Maybe I'll switch it up this time, with colored lights for a change ... but then, I do like those little white ones, they look so classy, plus I already have a bunch of those ... somewhere in my crafts' room.

Oh ... and all those extra fun gadgets I already bought this year, and mentioned in the Halloween story above? Since they're presents, they're already put in Christmas bags sitting under that tree, ready to be given at Christmas. WOW! That's a first! The tree's up and most of my local shopping's already done and bag-wrapped! Something positive for 2020!

* * *

THANKSGIVING AND CHRISTMAS TODAY
6 Nov 2020

Even though it's been exactly two months over 17 years since I initially wrote those two pieces, "just because", it was fun reading them again, and remembering the two specific days I wrote about. It made me realize that material things and Walmart and Michaels, haven't really changed that

35

much over the years, they've just gotten more expensive ... actually the only thing different is no more dropping off film to be developed. Now all the pictures are on my cell phone. But my crafts' room is still full of all those things discussed, some completed, some not.

We've just all gotten older, and instead of doing things for, or with, my grandkids, it's now the great-grands. The one major change in my life since writing those stories, is within the family: losing my husband, youngest sister and two granddaughters, the subsequent moves of nine of the remaining twelve grandkids to different states with their jobs, and the ensuing moves to those states, of four of our six kids after they retired, to be with some of their own kids and grands. (And we just found out number 15-great grandbaby is on the way, back in No Carolina.)

I much preferred it when all the kids were growing up at home, and bringing their friends over all the time, especially during Thanksgiving and Christmas. It was nothing to cook each year, for between 30 and 50 family members of all ages, neighbors, and friends, plus the occasional co-workers who had no family close-by.

It simply doesn't have the same feel, to go all-out and fix so much food for only the handful of family left in the area; not even as many as when I was cooking nightly meals for six kids, plus any friends they had over, and us, while the kids were growing up.

In addition to different areas of California, most of our kids, grandkids and greats are now scattered around in many states: Alaska, Nebraska, Oklahoma, Mississippi, North Carolina, Ohio, and the youngest, who just joined the Air Force, is currently in Virginia, waiting to be sent to her duty station the end of the year; most likely in Germany.

I used to love shopping for presents, but not anymore. I hate doing Christmas shopping since so many have moved; now it's mostly through Amazon, or other gift cards, for those living out of area, but one thing I've continued doing is making candy, lots of candy, and several different kinds; a variety of fudges and rocky roads, brittles, divinity and more. I hate sending presents through the mail, but I do make sure to send off boxes of colorful pink, mint green, white, peanut-butter brown, and chocolate chip shades of brown candy to each of the kids at Christmas, with their gift cards stuffed in the box.

Unfortunately for our kids and their progeny, very few even live in the same state, so they'll never be able to have the closeness with all the cousins, aunts and uncles, plus grandparents and greats, at gatherings, like my sisters and I did, my kids did, and the grandkids did, growing up. The younger ones, mainly, are missing out on so many fond memories and traditions of our large family during the holidays, especially helping Granny with the baking and candy-making for Thanksgiving and Christmas, playing with all their cousins, the traditional foods, love, and stories passed down from three generations. That's just sad, and they'll never know what they missed.

*　*　*

My first attempt at Haiku, during DST March, 2010, with the prompt for a critique group: *A Storm is Coming.* It's a holiday for some, correct? And this one comes twice a year, so we celebrate it twice. Sometimes happy about it, sometimes not. If you don't know what DST is, just read the Haiku.

DST: A STORM IS COMING

"A storm is coming"
Can't figure out what to do:
Can a cat Haiku?

Help! Look out below
Above, and everywhere
A storm is coming

Not the weather kind;
The Little Chickery-type
That young black kitty

Cat will kill it all
Necklace, tie, belt, shoelaces,
Anything that hangs

Cat opens drawers
Cat climbs inside the oven
Hides in kitchen sink

Cat toe, stuck in drain
Cat almost loses his claw,
Good thing Granny's there

Cat tries for ceiling
Instead, swings from curtain rod
Bedroom curtains fall

Cat falls in toilet
Cat jumps out, wet, runs around
Cat goes back for more

Knocks razors in tub
Razor in the kitten's mouth
Good thing Granny's there

Deer heads on the wall
Not for long, with demon-cat
Deer heads on the floor

Christmas tree still up
Cats can't go out, need to climb
Up and down they go

Climbs to top of tree
Scurry-cat climbs up there too
Fight at top … poor tree

Tree wins … still standing
Cats don't care, back up they go
Play-chase each other

Windy-cat's asleep
Not for long with Chickery;
Licks her ear ~ get up!

Returning favor
Windy gives cat thorough bath
That's not what cat wants

Dobby-cat's asleep
Chickery can't leave alone
Licks this cat's ears, too

Dobby chases cat
Play fight is on … run through house
This is what cat wants

Watch out in the dark
Kitten messing up throw rugs
Not where they should be

Kitty thinks he's smart
Kitten hides in rug-tunnels
Cat then tripped over

Tries to get away
Then back again ~ stupid cat
Will cat never learn

Cat jumps on bookcase
Knocks the lamp off and it breaks;
The light bulb and all

Cat goes back again
Breaks another bulb! Oh, no!
A storm is coming

Keeps me up at night
Cat jumps on and off the bed
From the window sill

Daylight Saving Time
Don't forget to change your clock
Lose an hour's sleep
                                    12 March 2010

Her baby sister called her Nonie, her great-granddaughter calls her GumGum. Norma Jean Thornton, AKA Noniedoodles, a multiple County and State Fair award-winning baker, candy-maker, art-doodler, plus award-winning writing granny from Rio Linda, California, creates her doodle-art and dabbles with her writings at the computer, with unwanted help from her feisty cats.

lulu.com/spotlight/nonie
lulu.com/spotlight/TheGrannysWritings
noniedoodles@yahoo.com
*"Love Never Dies" in Harlequin's Inspirational Anthology, A Kiss Under the Mistletoe
*Nonie's Big Bottom Girls' Rio Linda Cookbooks (4)
*Nonie's "Stuff" Cookbooks (Candy &...Stuff; Cookies...&...Stuff; Soups &...Stuff)
*Nosie Rosie's Diaries: (True cat diaries, written by The Granny & The Windy)
(Years 1 & 2 of 16-years)
*Nonie's Cat Anthologies (Fun, not-so-fun, sometimes crazy short cat stories) 2 Volumes
*Nonie's Wet Kitty Kisses Anthologies (Mostly humorous Shorts) 2 Volumes
*noniedoodles coloring books (artwork by Nonie's original doodles) Several Volumes
*Doodles the Dorky Dragon, in the Dorky Land of Noniedoodles
*Every 2019 & 2020 NCPA Anthology

THE LESSER MELON

M.L. HAMILTON

Every Christmas the family gathers to celebrate. Usually, we meet at my mother's house on Christmas Eve, then Christmas day is spent at my house. Almost every family gathering, no matter the occasion, is marked by a potluck. Every time I ask my mother what she wants me to bring, she tells me vegetables and dip.

Now I know that my crazy, busy life is the reason why she tells me this. She knows that with my work schedule and raising three boys, I don't have a lot of time to cook. And let's be honest, she knows I hate cooking even though I am relatively proficient at it. Usually, I am only too happy to bring my vegetables and dip, but this year, I felt I was up for a more challenging fare.

I told her I was off work and could bring something a bit more demanding. Of course, this is my mother, God love her, and so she gave me fruit salad. Fruit salad? In December? Really?

Suck it up, I told myself. You asked for this, I told myself. You couldn't keep your big mouth shut and be grateful for vegetables and dip, I told myself. And so, the day before Christmas I found myself in the local supermarket, trying to buy fruit for a fruit salad and not have to break out the credit cards to pay for it.

When I mentioned to my father how hard it was to find the requisite berries in December, he told me to get a cantaloupe. After all, everyone loves cantaloupe, he said. Cantaloupe, okay. I can find cantaloupe...I think...I hope. Not much of a fan myself, but it didn't seem like an overly summery kind of fruit.

I found a cantaloupe and ignored the stares of the other patrons buying more practical fare. It wasn't a particularly large or good-looking cantaloupe, but it felt soft. Coupled with oranges, bananas and apples I figured I'd have a perfectly respectable fruit salad come Christmas Eve.

I headed to the checkout counter and chose the self-check because I wanted out of the crowded store as quickly as possible. I frequently use self-check. I guess I'm something of a control freak, but it didn't occur to me that some things are better left for the professionals. There are no barcodes on cantaloupe. In fact, there are no stickers with a convenient number to enter into the computer.

I pressed the button that said Look up item. An alphabet scrolled down the right side of the screen and in the middle were helpful pictures of frequently bought items. I scanned over the frequently bought items, figuring cantaloupe might be there, but I didn't see a round, whitish-brown ball in any of the images. Not a problem, I told myself, for just to the right was the alphabet waiting for me to press. Logically, I pressed C.

A list of many C items came scrolling across the screen. I searched through the CAs, but found no cantaloupe. In fact, the only C vegetable (beyond carrot) was Casaba melon. Casaba? Not cantaloupe? In that moment, I heard Jerry Seinfeld's voice in my head. Casaba? Casaba melon under C? Casaba is a lesser melon.

And then enter doubt. Do I know how to spell cantaloupe? Maybe I don't. When have I ever had the occasion to spell it? Maybe it isn't spelled with a C, maybe...just maybe, it's spelled with a K. Glancing around sheepishly to be sure no one was looking, I pressed the K to M button. At the very bottom were the words melon, cantaloupe. Now it's stupid to feel relief over something so ridiculous, but I was so grateful I wasn't going to have to summon one of the harried salesclerks to tell her that I didn't know how to find cantaloupe in her computer.

Ringing up a $3.99 melon brought me back to the reason I was here. Tonight when I go to my mother's house for Christmas Eve, I will present her with the most expensive fruit salad I've ever made and in my head will be Jerry Seinfeld's voice saying, "At least you didn't settle for a lesser melon."

 In 2010, ML Hamilton made her first New Year's resolution – to get serious about her writing. That same year she found a publisher, Wild Wolf Publications, in England and became a traditionally published author. After five years with Wild Wolf, she decided to venture out on her own into the exciting world of self-publishing. Since that time, she's published 56 novels, written an award-winning screenplay and sold more than 270,000 eBooks.

A full-time schoolteacher and mother of three grown sons, ML carves out time to write in the evenings, weekends and during breaks. Her most popular series, the Peyton Brooks Mysteries, is set in her hometown of San Francisco. The Peyton Brooks Mysteries have been in the top 100 on Amazon for over a year and have reached number 2 in the U.S. and number 1 in the United Kingdom, Australia, and Canada in the Mystery Anthology category.

MY JOY
ROSEMARY COVINGTON MORGAN

Holla shout jump cry
Dance around the living room
Headstands cartwheels splits flips
Feel like you can fly

Flour sugar butter cream
Nutmeg vanilla cinnamon
Mama Grandma Papa
And your very best friend

Brothers sisters cousins
Aunts uncles friends and kids
All 'round the dinner table
Stories lies tales fables

Smiling laughing tickles
Giggle 'til you choke
Nose lips twitch wiggle
Silly stupid funny joke

Fireplace wine book
Music in your ears
Eyelids droop doze sleep
Comfy reading chair.

Christmas Easter Halloween
Springtime flowers Ice Cream
Children believe fairy tales
Bright eyes twinkling things

Stars moon green grass sun
Warmth cold rain and snow
All those things said before
Add excitement merriment endless fun

JOY!

A KAPOHO CHRISTMAS
FRANCES KAKUGAWA

It was Christmas without lights.
It was Christmas without indoor plumbing.
It was Christmas without carolers at the window
Muffed and warm under falling snow.

But there was Christmas.

A Christmas program at school
The Holy Night reenacted:
White tissue paper glued on spines of coconut fronds
Shaped as angel wings and haloes.
Long white bathrobes, over bare feet.

The plantation manager with a bagful of candies
His annual role in the village where he reigned.
Fathers in Sunday best
After a hard day's work in sugar cane fields.
Mothers in dresses fashioned after Sears catalogs.
Children, restless, on wooden benches,
Waiting for Santa's jolly Ho Ho Ho.

A fir tree from the hills,
Needles not lasting 24 hours.
Chains from construction paper,
Origami balls and strands of tin-foiled tinsel.
Kerosene and gas lamps
Moving shadows on the walls.

It was not the Christmas of my dreams.
No carolers at the window,
Singing Silent Night, Holy Night.
No large presents under a real Christmas tree

No fireplaces and rooftop chimneys.
No blue-eyed boy handing me hot chocolate.

For 18 years, the true Christmas
Lived in my head until Madame Pele
Came to my rescue from Kilauea crater
And buried our kerosene lamps
Under red hot lava.

Finally! I said, without a backward glance,
Running out fast in bare feet
On unpaved roads
To the Christmas of my dreams.

 An award winning internationally published author of sixteen books, Frances has received numerous awards from literary and family caregiving organizations – among them, The Hawai'i Book Publishers Association, Northern CA Publishers and Authors, Mom's Choice Awards, Sunrise Ministry Foundation, CA Writers' Club and the Hawai'i Gerontological Society.

Frances has been recognized by the Hawai'i Japanese Women's Society Foundation as one of the Outstanding Women of the 20th Century in Hawai'i. She was a columnist for the Hawai'i Herald – the "Dear Frances" advice column for caregivers – and gives lectures, workshops and readings to schools and conferences nationwide on the subjects of caregiving, teaching, writing, children's literature and poetry.

Her work has appeared in various anthologies. Two of her children's books have been made into musical stage productions. Frances also facilitates a poetry writing support group for caregivers in Sacramento, Ca, where she lives.

THE AFRICAN CELEBRATION OF KWANZAA

VICKI WARD "NYANYA"

A Holiday for All Seasons

S hortly before my birth, my grandmother adopted the Swahili term for Grandmother, Nyanya, as a name for her grandchildren to call her. She linked our heritage and her revered responsibility, to be called this name by all of her grandchildren and now by the great-grandchildren. I continue to call her by Nyanya, that esteemed name.

Story narrated by *Dorian Ward* (16-year-old grandson of Nyanya, AKA Vicki)

Family Thanksgiving Dinner

Ah, Thanksgiving dinner with the *entire* family! Thank God for the cooks who prepared that beautiful spread! Thankfully, each cook had a specialty in our family, and just as on past occasions, they did not disappoint! From the adult table to the several children's tables, after dinner, everyone sought their refuge, their place to lay back and digest some of the best food they recalled eating since the last year's feast.

They needed time to hide away while turkey, dressing, ham, mashed potatoes and gravy, yams, homemade dinner rolls, and more lulled them into total submission. The children were already outdoors, and the young adults were also somewhere outside, off doing their own thing. The men watched football, so the living-room was full of testosterone as they each shouted for the victory or defeat of one team or the other.

After about an hour of separate spaces, Nyanya called

for everyone to gather in the family room for an announcement. The whispers and questions began immediately, everyone asking others what was up. Once everyone was gathered together tightly in the family room and hallways, Nyanya stood up to speak.

"Family, we have Celebrated Kwanzaa much the same each year. I wanted to wait to announce that there would be changes to the Kwanzaa Program this year."

Everyone knew this was a major holiday event she prepared for and staged in her home each year. What a bomb that announcement was! She waited until the family Thanksgiving dinner to announce that the Kwanzaa Celebration would be different this year. There was gasping, and a rumble of noise that sounded like a dozen unfinished sentences jumbled together. No one knew what to make of her announcement.

Uncle Drue was the first to speak. "Are you canceling the Celebration this year?"

She took a long, whimsical look around the room, eyeing everyone, with all eyes locked in on her. She threw her head back and laughed out loud, watching the shocked faces. Still smiling, she looked around the room again, slowly, making eye contact with each family member before speaking. She told of a new vision for our Kwanzaa Celebration. She talked about traditions; about how older family members teach the younger ones to assume more responsibility. She reminded family elders and youth that this was a natural course of life, assigning new tasks with more responsibility to the children as they matured.

Nyanya stated she would continue in her role as *Chief Kwanzaa Coordinator*, pausing long enough to show a sly smile, easing some of the room's tension, and said she would continue hosting the celebration at her home. She told the family she had created task charts for assignments and asked them to respond to her indicating their preference. She stressed she wanted our Kwanzaa Celebration to become a more significant source of pride for the younger family members, creating another joyous family gathering that held meaning now and for future generations.

The next day, they realized she had thoroughly thought this out because each adult received a Kwanzaa Celebration Planning Worksheet in their email, detailing the celebration's vital information, music, songs, speakers, poetry, food, and programs.

Aunt Ellen responded with a snarky email stating, "It's not like we're producing a Hollywood movie!"

Well, that broke the ice, injecting some humor at the right time. The worksheet demonstrated Nyanya's organizational and planning skills. All tasks were included, including those she never relinquished:

- Food Committee—Solicit donations of food and desserts from family and friends, supply plates and utensils, setting up the feast table, and cleanup
- Entertainment-- Seek speaker, music, songs, musicians, poets,
- History Organization -- Print programs, create and hang posters
- Ceremonial components -- Ensure all are in working order
- Seating--Determine the number of guests; order additional chairs

When I saw the email, I couldn't stop smiling. It was finally my chance to do more in the Kwanzaa Celebration! I texted the older cousins and asked if they read the email and what they thought of it. There was very little response, but the few responses I received contained one word: NO.

Arden, Donavon, Trenice, Aleah, and Donnell were the first to tell their parents they wanted to work on the Kwanzaa program. Nyanya told one of my aunts after one week, with no word, she was hurt and almost in tears at the lack of interest. Reluctantly, she decided to allow the new ideas to simmer awhile longer, giving the family time to digest this new plan.

Well, the cavalry, in the form of wise parents, came to the rescue. My mom Toria, and my Dad Donnell called a parents' only meeting. They reminded everyone how much Nyanya enjoyed celebrating Kwanzaa in her home and had done so for a long while, with little assistance. Dad reminded them that from the beginning, she invited family and friends to share in the celebration and only half of the family attended, yet, she continued gaining knowledge, still holding it in her home. She added additional content, guest speakers, drumming, songs, and more as the attendance grew to over 40 people.

My cousins' parents also began talking to them. Within days, there was a unanimous decision by the adults. All of the youth in every age group would take part, no matter how small, in the program's staging. They discussed that the adults would assume more duties, taking some of the load from Nyanya and make this a real Family Kwanzaa Celebration from now on. For several days the parents held meetings among themselves as well as with their children.

Nyanya couldn't wait for too long; the slow speed the wheels of change turned were making her anxious and tense. She believed her idea had fallen on deaf ears, time was of the essence, and she needed to move on. Finally, my dad called and told her about the parents' holding meetings. He told her the family was taking their cues from her and acting on her lead.

Nyanya called me to come to her home, and we went for a walk. She began talking about changes in the ceremony. She knew I would be anxious to hear about them since I had been bugging her for more responsibility at our Kwanzaa Celebration. At the end of our walk, we sat down, and she questioned me about the significance of Kwanzaa.

She asked questions I could not respond to, even though I thought I remembered most of the principles. With a stern face, never giving me an indication of whether I had answered correctly or not, she continued asking questions. I just kept thinking about what I learned from her and other elders over the years. Her final question was, "Dorian do you believe you have the spirit of your ancestors and that they will be proud of you?"

I quickly answered an excited, "Yes!"

She beamed a broad smile, threw open her arms, and said, "Then you have matured enough to take on the role of

Master of Ceremonies!"

I jumped into her arms, and the two of us hugged each other tightly, laughing together.

Our whole family: aunts, uncles, and children talked about the Kwanzaa Celebration, the children taking direction from the elders, talking excitedly about what we expected that day.

The Seven Principles of Kwanzaa

- *Umoja:* means unity in Swahili. "To strive for and maintain unity in the family, community, nation, and race."
- *Kujichagulia*: or self-determination. This principle refers to defining, naming, creating, and speaking for oneself.
- *Ujima*: Translated as "collective work and responsibility," refers to uplifting your community.
- *Ujamaa*: Collective economics.
- *Nia*: Purpose
- *Kuumba*: "creativity," To do always as much as we can, in the way we can, in order to leave our community more beautiful and beneficial than we inherited it.
- *Imani:* The final principle translates to "faith"

Our Family Kwanzaa Celebration!

Nyanya is always excited yet calm hosting the Kwanzaa Celebration, and insists we are timely. It was still early; and we in charge were all instructed to come early to ensure everything was displayed and arranged correctly. We each took this to heart, and most everyone helping had arrived at her home several hours before the guests would begin arriving. We all laughed at the front door, nodding to each other knowingly, to see Nyanya had already placed a large sign on the front door welcoming guests to our *Kwanzaa Celebration* with the greeting: *Habari Gani!* (What's the News?)

A steady stream of guests soon began arriving. There

was a warming current of celebration throughout the house, amid the greetings and hugs. Several young cousins were assigned to greet the guests, give them programs detailing *Kwanzaa's* observance and historical significance, and show them to their seats. Within the next hour, the house was beyond capacity. Thinking quickly, the teens and younger kids began creating a circle of chairs along the great room walls encircling the presentation table to accommodate the additional guests coming in.

Nyanya walked through each room to ensure the cousins were engaging with the guests. I knew we would be starting soon and kept glancing over to where she was. She looked over at me and gave the nod to begin the celebration. I nodded to Khalid to hold the drumming. I turned to the older teens standing at the table, signaling the official start of our *Kwanzaa Celebration.*

Dorian's Welcome

Habari Gani!
They enthusiastically respond with the traditional general response: *"njema."* However, the Kwanzaa's greeting response may be different for a specific day, if the event is celebrated daily from December 26th to December 31st.

"We welcome you to the annual Kwanzaa Celebration of *United Family* of the *Wards, Smith's, and Brown's.* We invite you to sit back and celebrate our history and culture. We want to expand your knowledge about our ancestors and ourselves. Today, we will learn about our heritage, make personal commitments, and learn to appreciate our gifts.

"Our Celebration includes food for the mind as well as food to nourish your stomachs. We will celebrate our harvest and our children, who are our future. Today, we will honor our ancestors and close the Celebration with a *Karamu* (the Feast) for all to join in, celebrating our past, present, and future.

"Thank you for joining us celebrating Kwanzaa today.

We thank you for sharing in celebrating our families, our community, and our people."

(Khalid resumes drumming.) The youth begin placing objects that have symbolic meaning to Africa's culture on the table.

Dorian identifies each of the objects and their significance to African Life and Culture.

D'Mari: First, we drape the **Bendera**, the Black National Flag, over the table.

Sharleese placed the **Mkeka,** a large straw mat, to hang over the table, symbolizing our African traditions and history.

Donavon placed the **Kinara,** the candle holder (for seven candles), which symbolizes the continent of Africa, our place of origin, and roots.

- **Mishumaa Saba**-- the seven candles, 1 Black, 3 Red, 3 Green, symbolize the seven principles of Kwanzaa

·Donnell inserted the black candle

·Aleah inserted a red candle

·Arden placed a red candle

·Darryl placed a green candle

·Jalen placed a green candle

·Alicia placed the final red candle

·Sharleese added the last green candle

- **Mazao,** the crops, symbolize Kwanzaa's historical roots as a harvest-type first fruits celebration. D'Mari added apples and oranges to the table.
- **Muhundi** or **Vibunzi,** symbolize offspring. Jalen offered corn
- **Kikombe Cha Umoja Unity Cups** symbolize the First Principle of Kwanzaa and is used for pouring Libation. Sharleese placed these on the table
- **Nguzo Saba Poster**, The Seven Principles Poster. Donavon added the poster which details the key role they play in Kwanzaa
- **Zawadi Gifts,** African history-culture books and/or heritage symbols, symbolize the key role of

education, culture and faith in Kwanzaa. Dorian added these.

- **Green Plants** symbolize the "oneness" between Africans and Nature. Nyanya placed the plants on the table.
- **Other Decorations employing the African Motif** - Art Pieces, candles, flags, pictures, and our national colors (RED, BLACK & GREEN) are displayed throughout the home, creating an Afrocentric atmosphere. Moms and Dads of all children have added mementos, photos of parents now deceased, bibles, and other African memorabilia with special meaning to the table.

I looked over at Nyanya. She was beaming with pride. The older cousins and the younger ones executed their jobs well in the presence of our veteran Kwanzaa Leader. Now, I understand some of what she went through. I know it took commitment and lots of patience. We had to walk just a few steps in her shoes to understand how she did it and why. Ultimately, it was for our growth to nurture and hold in our hearts, to recognize and understand African culture, to better understand ourselves.

Gather My People
Dorian Ward

Gather my people,
Gather for me
Though suffered long,
Your weakness grows strong
Come young, come old,
Come as you are

Gather my people,
The journey is long
Dancing, praising,
Singing robust songs,
Hear again, voices from the past
Celebrate our harvest,

Our daughters, our sons

Gather my people,
In celebration of life
With libations lifted
To honor our ancestors
Nurturing our own,
Remembering our strife
My people can't afford
To quit in this life

Gather my people,
Our fate guided by God
With searching eyes look up
See the vision at last
United in love, rise to the challenge,
Awaken each morning,
To a fresh new canvas

Gather my people
remember your past
Protect that which is now.

Gather my people
With an eye toward beyond
Remember my people,
Our struggle as one

Gather my people, gather to me,
Come sing, and dance,
Create and make new
Fear not the unknown,
Forging a great bond

Gather my people,
Our struggle as one.

Nyanya came forward to lead the final portion of the Kwanzaa Celebration; The Pouring of Libations with the

Kikombe Cha Umoja Unity Cups.

She explained The Pouring of Libation is a spiritual and venerable act that has its roots in traditional African societies. This act symbolizes the First Principle of Kwanzaa. The children distributed cups to all in attendance. Libation is poured to honor the ancestors, who have gone before us, yet who remain spiritually active in our lives. By actively remembering our parents and grandparents and other loved ones we ensure that they are not forgotten, emphasizing that their lives had meaning.

The youth have poured water into the guest's cups. They walk to the *Bendera*, where a large vase sits, into which they pour libations honoring ancestors, calling out names of parents, grandparents, and others who had gone on before them yet were not forgotten and remained with them in spirit. Once done, they returned to their seat

Closing the Kwanzaa Ceremony

Nyanya

"Today, we have all borne witness to the evolution, growth, and sustaining of African people. You now hold the knowledge of strong-willed people, of people committed to values taught and handed down by ancestors. Their strength and commitment, their will to endure, and to prosper are forever with us. Look around you. You are witness to our love and work, our struggle, and our endurance. Today, you have gained invaluable information about your history, the incredible strength, fortitude, and the evolving spirit and growth of people birthed from the mother country, Africa. Come, let's complete our Celebration, enjoying the Feast of our unity in recognition of our ancestors and in anticipation of our future!"

Vicki Ward is an award-winning author. Her award-winning books include *Life's Spices from Seasoned Sistahs,* and *More of Life's Spices; Sistahs Keepin' It Real.* Each volume provides insight into the lives of women from different countries and cultures, how they live, love, celebrate triumphs, support, and nurture their families. Another award-winning book she authored is *Savvy Sassy and Bold After 50, a Midlife Re-birth,* which highlights maturing women whose needs change dramatically after 50. Her research shows these women *now* put themselves first! Affirmed with new insights, they charter unique lifestyles focused on new goals. Her latest book is *Supercharge Your Life After 60; 10 Tips to Navigate a Dynamic Decade*; a guide for those navigating life after 60, with aging bodies, additional health challenges, considering retirement or caring for aging parents. It is an excellent resource for those aging beyond 60.

Visit her website at www.vickiward.net.

ALL IS CALM

JACKIE ALCALDE MARR

Lights twinkle brightly
Snowflakes fall silent to earth
Inside all is calm

Hearth is still glowing
Milk and cookies awaiting
Magic hooves on roof

Dreams of sugarplums
Bedraggled parents tip-toe
Sprinkling their sweet love

Morning is gleeful
Wadded paper and ribbons
Fortunate loved ones

Surprises and laughs
Flurry of fabulous play
Outside all is calm

THE ORNAMENTS
SCOTT CHARLES

C hristmas season always reminds me of my mother. Her birthday, in April, may occasionally slip by me, but come December memories of her abound, thanks largely to her insatiable creative streak.

To explain how that relates to Christmas, you need the full picture of my mother's creativity. She painted, she etched, cut and assembled, glued and pasted, using plastics, yarn, clay, you name it. She took discarded relics, pieced them together, and made new relics. From needlepoint to macramé, sewing to ceramics, she left no craft stone unturned.

Eventually, her ambition led her to pottery, and that became her most prolific endeavor. She bought a kiln, a big old thing, then a smaller one for good measure. The bigger kiln was so big it required more space and electricity than what we had, so she sold one house and bought another in order to set up a workshop in a small utility shed. She didn't use a potter's wheel; instead she bought molds or raw clay that was already prepared for baking. In addition to scores of macramé belts, hot pads, hanging plant holders, and assorted other tchotchkes, she churned out hundreds of hand-painted clay trivets, pots, mugs, and ceramic animals

Eventually, my mother got too old to live in a big house by herself, so we moved her to a smaller house and stored all the craft utensils, including the kilns.

Eventually. even a small house was too big, and she moved into a small apartment closer to my wife and me.

And, eventually, she died.

Besides confronting decisions over what to do with her furniture and assorted bric-a-brac, I found myself conflicted over Mom's creative legacy. What was I going to do with all those finished crafts as well as works-in-progress and supplies, including paints, yarns, glues, needles, and paint brushes, not to mention the darn kilns?

I decided the supplies should be passed on to a local community center that ran an arts program for people with disabilities. Luckily, I also found someone to take the kilns. But that still left me with hundreds more items, large and small: furniture, silverware, mirrors, wooden frames, a few small antiques, and hundreds of ceramic pots, trivets, cups, mugs, plates, and figurines.

Yet all that paled in comparison to what turned out to be my mother's true specialty, at least if you judge it by volume: Christmas ornaments. These creations represented by far her largest output. She left behind enough ornaments to decorate a whole neighborhood of Christmas trees. And each one bore a special imprint: her initials.

I already had a couple dozen ornaments my mother had made and sent along over the years. Some displayed a high level of artistic ability, and some were childishly simple. But every one, no matter how simple or complex, held a little bit of my mother's desire to do good work. Each one represented her attempt to imbue an inanimate object with a little bit of hope, a little bit of sunshine, and love.

In other words, it made my mother happy to create these objects, and she hoped other people would be happy to have them. Even items she made from material that was inexpensive or from a thrift shop, or from a discard pile, no matter how humble, my mother would turn those discards into something interesting and fun, and each one held a bit of charm peculiar to itself.

So, I decided to have a yard sale. I wanted to have my hand on each object, smile at the person who bought it, and tell them my mother made it. And turn the object around so they could see where she had imprinted her initials, "O.C." I wanted the transaction to be personal.

On Friday evening, my wife and I set up tables in the front yard and started putting items out. We wanted to start bright and early Saturday morning. We actually made a few sales that evening as people who happened to be out and about noticed what we were doing.

Saturday morning a friend and I went out early to post our yard-sale signs while my wife and a couple of other friends finished the set-up in the front yard and driveway. It was turning into a beautiful day. With our friends and neighbors hanging out with us, it had the air of a social event too.

I had decided on rock-bottom prices for this yard sale, not out of disrespect for my mother's talent, but I wanted people to enjoy getting a bargain. Sure, there were a few large items that pulled in a little more, like a recliner that sold for $75, and some antique wooden frames that went for $10 or $15 apiece. But most everything else sold for loose change or maybe a dollar.

We were inundated with shoppers. Besides having tons of stuff for sale, word of my pricing strategy must have spread. Plus, everyone was having fun. We even made a decent sum, which I thought was a hoot.

But the big thing, the thing that really made me happy, the thing that put a little sunshine in my life, was knowing that all those Christmas ornaments had found a home. Hundreds of them. Little angels and elves and stars and Santas. Reindeer and candy canes. Lace snowflakes and ceramic wreaths. And somewhere on each one the initials "O.C."

You know how it is when you toss a pebble into a pond? Even a small pebble makes ripples.

Every Christmas when we decorate, we have quite a number of ornaments to choose from, many from my mother's collection. For each ornament, I carefully choose a spot for it that highlights its particular charms. In doing so, I'm reminded that elsewhere there are other people who are also hanging up ornaments that my mother made.

And maybe, just maybe, every once in a while, they notice her initials. Even if they don't know what the O.C. stands for, they take a little pleasure from what she made. They know that somebody made this, one step at a time, with their own hands, as an expression of joy. And it makes them happy. It makes me happy too.

Somewhere out there this holiday season, it also makes my mother happy.

 Scott Charles was born in the Midwest and relocated to Sacramento, California in the 1980s. He lives a happy life with his wife and his dog. He has just released a novel, "*The Illustrated Hen*," which is available on Amazon.com. He is also the author of several plays, including "*Dinners With Augie*." You can see some of his other works on his website at www.libernetics.com.

THE UNEXPECTED HOLIDAY SURPRISE

CHARLENE JOHNSON

"I'm so glad we were able to find this beautiful property close to your parents." Felicity sipped her coffee at the dinette table in the sunroom, gazing out the bay window overlooking the forest behind their log cabin. "It's so peaceful here."

"Yes, and we were lucky to find a cabin the size we wanted that required some upgrades but nothing we couldn't handle," Dex added. "It was nice to work with my dad and my brothers on the projects."

"I can't wait for my family to see it."

Dex chuckled. "I'm sure your brother will be less inclined to take a walk in the forest again after what happened during the Christmas holiday at my parents' house."

"It's been two years. Bobby should be over it by now. After the tongue lashing your mom gave your brothers, I doubt they'll terrorize my brother again."

"I keep hoping those two will grow up soon. I was working and owned a house by the time I was their age."

Felicity slapped his arm playfully. "Cut them a break. They just turned twenty. They are still big kids. From what you told me your parents spoiled them."

"My parents did indulge them shamelessly, but they are good kids. Both are in college studying forestry and are doing well."

"Is the college close enough to the forest for them to shift?"

"Yes. Green River College is situated on a bluff overlooking the Big Soos Creek and Green River Valley. There is an expansive forest with many hiking trails. It's quite beautiful. We'll have to go there one weekend and surprise them."

Felicity nodded. "That would be fun."

Dex took her hand. "Speaking of fun, I have a surprise for you."

Her eyes lit up. "What kind of surprise?"

"We're going to Leavenworth for the weekend. I made reservations at one of the local hotels. We leave in the morning."

She clapped her hands. "I've been wanting to go there. I saw a video of last year's Christmas festivities on YouTube. What made you think of it? I never mentioned it to you."

"I know how much you love Christmas. My parents took us there many times as kids and we all loved it. I thought you would too."

"I can't wait." Felicity stood up.

"Where are you going?" Dex asked. "You haven't finished your breakfast."

She leaned over and kissed him. "I'm too excited to eat. I have to start packing."

* * *

Leavenworth, Washington, is a small town filled with Bavarian architecture. It could have been featured in a *Hallmark Christmas* movie with all the smells, sounds and festive, merry atmosphere. It was hard not to feel the excitement in the air. The clip-clop of the horses' hooves, jingle bells and Christmas music create a unique symphony. The explosion of multi-colored twinkle lights and newly fallen snow brought the street and storefronts to life. The sidewalks teemed with tourists weaving in and out of the unique boutiques. Against the clear moonlit sky, the Sleeping Lady Mountain could be seen on the horizon.

"What a magical place, Dex," Felicity gushed with excitement, her arm looped through his as they strolled leisurely down Front Street past the park where families were sledding.

"I knew you would like it here," Dex replied. "It's a great way for us to kick off the holiday season."

"I want to go into every shop and look around. There's so much to see."

"We could do that, but it would take hours and we still need to eat dinner."

"Why don't we eat first and then shop," Felicity compromised. "I'm hungry too."

They chose the *Stein Leavenworth* with its communal seating and amazing fifty-five beers on tap. It was a minute walk from the park. Dex ordered the Beer Braised Bratwurst Plate and Felicity had the Sasquatch Baby Back Rib Rack meal. For dessert they both ordered a *Stein Root Beer* Float.

"I'm stuffed," Dex patted his stomach. "I need to walk off the large amount of food I ate and the beer I drank."

"I couldn't eat all my meal, though I tried," Felicity added. "We'll have to come back here tomorrow night."

"I wouldn't mind trying more of those great beers."

They left the restaurant and strolled down the street, going into multiple shops, but their attention was drawn to *Front Street Park* where peals of laughter and shouts of joy echoed up and down the busy street.

"Let's go watch the sledders," Felicity said.

"What about shopping?" Dex asked.

"We can shop tomorrow."

Front Street Park was filled with people. Some were enjoying the music and grand light displays and throwing snowballs, while others were busy sledding down the hill in the middle of the park. When they reached the bottom of the hill, they collected their sleds and ran back up to the top to do it all over again.

The trunks and branches of trees were wrapped in colorful twinkle lights and a large wooden gazebo, adorned with Christmas lights and garland, looked top heavy with fluffy white snow.

Dex and Felicity bought steaming cups of hot chocolate and settled onto one of the wooden benches scattered throughout the park.

"We should have brought our sleds," Dex said as he

sipped his chocolate.

"Next time," Felicity replied. "I think we should make a weekend here an annual thing. I'd love to bring my family. They'd love it here."

They watched the children speed down the hill on their sleds. Some kids were bundled in snowsuits and others in thick hooded coats and gloves in a kaleidoscope of bright colors.

The sudden sound of raised voices caught Dex and Felicity's attention and not in a good way. A circle of children at the top of the hill were taunting a boy and girl who stood silently, not reacting to the harsh words.

"Where's your sled, Mikey?" a boy in the blue snowsuit asked, his voice filled with disapproval.

"We don't have one," Mikey replied evenly, dressed in a brown tattered wool coat and jeans, his eyes furtively looking around for a way to escape. "We just came to watch."

"If you don't have a sled, you don't belong here."

"You can't stop me and my brother from being here, Steven," a little girl, dressed in a worn pink coat standing by her brother replied. "It's a public park."

The boy named Steven pushed her. "We don't want you here, Jessica."

"Don't touch my sister," Mikey warned Steven as he advanced on him.

His sister grabbed his arm. "Don't, Mikey. It's alright. Ignore him. He's nothing but a bully."

"Yeah, get out of here," another one of the boys ordered.

"Can't your parents afford a sled?" yelled another boy standing beside Steven.

"That's none of your business." Jessica crossed her arms over her coat and lifted her chin.

"Where did you get the ugly pink coat? *Goodwill*?" a girl with white earmuffs and white down jacket jeered.

"Let's go, Jessica," Mikey said.

Jessica stomped her foot. "No, Mikey. I don't want to go."

"We have to. Mom and Dad will be worried."

"Ok," she replied, disappointed. She turned to glare at the kids still surrounding them and moved forward, pushing her way through them. Mikey followed her.

"Don't come back, losers."

Jessica and Mikey ignored Steven and headed down the hill and out of the park.

"How cruel. I wonder where they live?" Felicity whispered. "I can't put my finger on it but there's something different about them."

"They're shifters like us," Dex replied.

"You knew that?"

"Yes, I sensed it."

"I wish I was that perceptive."

"I've been around shifters my whole life. You haven't. You will be able to detect shifters in time."

"One thing I don't understand, Dex. You seemed surprised when I first shifted at your house."

He shrugged. "I can't explain it and that baffled me for a while. It's not like me not to recognize another shifter but I'd been watching the owl for weeks in my fox form and was so captivated by its relentless pursuit of the squirrel family. Perhaps that clouded my judgement. I'd spent so much time in the forest, seeing nothing but true animals for months, the idea of the owl being a shapeshifter never occurred to me. And when the owl was shot and I feared it would die, my only instinct was to save the beautiful creature." He took her hand. "Maybe it was something much deeper, I'll never know. There is something I do know implicitly, saving that amazing owl was the best decision I ever made."

Felicity smiled. "I'm glad you did too."

The shouts of the kids still on the hill caught their attention.

Felicity pointed to them. "What about them? Are they human?"

"Yes, strictly human," Dex answered.

"Hey, do you mind if we follow Mikey and Jessica?" Felicity asked. "It might sound intrusive, but I'd like to meet their parents and see if we can help them."

Dex nodded. "As long as you understand they might be hesitant to trust us and could refuse our help."

Dex and Felicity kept at a leisurely pace, not wanting to scare Mikey and Jessica, as they headed to the waterfront.

"Where do you think they're going?" she asked.

"It appears to the bridge that leads to Black Island."

"Do you think they live there?"

"It's a possibility."

Felicity and Dex waited until the kids hurried across the bridge and onto the island, disappearing into the forest.

They thought about shifting to follow them, but decided to find the kids' destination without doing so, not knowing what they might find. They would rely on their inherent enhanced senses to guide them. There were no hikers this time of the evening, but they traveled parallel to the hiking trail just in case.

Dex and Felicity walked past downed trees, and up elevated terrain, as the thicket of large trees grew dense.

"The kids know where they are going," Dex whispered.

"I agree," Felicity replied in a low voice.

Behind a jumble of large boulders and circle of redwoods, they saw the kids enter a camp. A man added wood to an open fire as a woman sat in a folding chair in front of it. A large tarp secured to nearby trees hovered above them, protecting them from the elements. Sleeping bags were stacked in a corner of the canopy.

"We're back," Mikey announced as he and Jessica approached them.

The woman smiled. "Good. Your dad and I were starting to worry."

"I wish you two would stop going into town," the man admonished. "We need to keep a low profile. What if you were followed?"

"Those stupid town's kids never follow us," Jessica snorted. "They're just a brunch of bullies."

He turned to Mikey and Jessica, and frowned. "Trouble with the kids again?"

Mikey shrugged. "They made fun of us like they always do. We're used to it."

"You might be, Mikey," Jessica said with disapproval. "I'm not. I wanted to punch Steven in the nose."

"Your mother and I don't condone violence, Jess, you know that," her father chided. "We can't afford to draw any attention. If the forestry department knew we are staying here, they might force us to leave. We don't have anywhere to go."

Jessica looked instantly apologetic. "I'm sorry, Daddy. Those kids are so mean. Why don't they like us?"

Her father shrugged. "It's the nature of some people. Not everyone is going to like you and those that don't, aren't important. It's the world we live in."

"Your dad's right," their mother agreed. "Not all kids are like the ones in town. Once we get settled, it will be different."

"When will that be?" Jessica questioned.

"It will be soon, Jess, I promise," her father answered as his eyes met his wife's.

"They're homeless," Felicity whispered.

"That's unfortunate," Dex agreed. "Let's go talk to them. Maybe there's something we can do to help them."

Dex took Felicity's hand and they entered the camp. "Good evening," he greeted.

Startled, the family turned to them, fear and panic on their faces. The man moved forward in front of his family, his stance defensive.

"What do you want?" he demanded.

"We don't mean to intrude," Dex said in a pleasant voice. "We just want to talk."

"What about? Are you the authorities? We've done nothing wrong."

"Nothing like that."

"We are tourists," Felicity added.

"Then why are you here? "Did you follow my kids?"

"I admit my wife and I did follow them, but not for what you think." Dex patted his chest. "We are shifters too."

The man remained wary as he studied them, his face serious. "I know what you are but not all shifters are well intentioned. I have to protect my family."

"I understand completely," Dex said. "My father has always been very protective of us. Surely, you can sense we mean no harm."

After a tense moment, the man relaxed and grinned. "I don't sense harm from you. Sorry. We're not used to seeing our kind in this forest."

"I've been there myself," Dex concurred. He pulled Felicity closer. "Hunters shot my wife when she was in the form of a great horned owl and I took her home to heal. Detecting other shifters is something I've known how to do most of my life, but I was so worried about saving the owl, I didn't realize she was a shifter until she revealed herself. When she did, I was more than elated." He gazed down at her, love in his eyes. "The rest is history."

The man grinned and extended his hand. "That's quite a love story. I'm Robert."

"Dex, and my wife, Felicity."

"This is my wife, Mary, and our children, Mikey and Jessica."

"So nice meeting you all," Felicity replied. "Jessica reminds me of myself when I was her age. She's a tough cookie, standing up to those kids trying to bully her and her brother."

"Mikey is always the peacemaker," Jessica replied matter-of-factly. "I'm not. I wanted to kick those kids' butts. Especially Steven. He's their leader."

"I should have let her," Mikey admitted sheepishly. "But she's my baby sister. We can't risk causing trouble."

"We didn't start it," Jessica countered.

"We never do, Jess."

"Mikey's right," Robert agreed. "We are too vulnerable."

"We don't mean to pry but why are you are staying on this island?" Felicity asked.

Robert sighed. "I lost my job earlier in the year and we were evicted from the cabin we were living in outside of Peshastin. I was a handyman for a local bed and breakfast. As the travel has slacked off due to the Covid-19 pandemic, the owner had to let me go." He paused. "Mr. Harris and his wife didn't want to let me go but had to close the B & B. They

73

are up in age and have decided to sell it. We've been living here deep in these woods trying to avoid the forest rangers and tourists for months. It's been relatively safe. There is a family of bears and a few solitary cougars and bobcats in the area. They keep most people away. We've been able to coexist with them in peace. They know we are more like them than humans."

"I understand," Dex said. "The main conflicts my family has had over the years are with humans. My parents' property is bookended by land owned by the state, so they get stray hunters on their property from time to time, even with No Trespassing signs posted."

"Exposure is always an underlying threat we have to live with," Robert said. "It's only temporary until I can find work elsewhere and get Mikey and Jess enrolled in school."

Mary patted her rounded stomach. "I hope we can find a permanent place soon with a new baby coming."

"How have you been surviving out here?" Dex asked.

"We catch salmon along the shore. Most we eat ourselves, but I have also been supplying fish to an old couple, the Barkers, who live nearby, outside of town. I was out fishing on the other side of the island when I heard someone fall into the water not far from where I was fishing. I went to investigate since I wasn't used to people being on that side of the island. Mr. Barker was struggling to stand up. I noticed a cut on his head. He told me he slipped and hit his head on a rock when he tried to wade out farther into the water. I took him home and told him I would bring him salmon so he didn't have to risk falling again. He and his wife have a large organic garden on their property, and they give me fruit and vegetables in exchange for the salmon. I take some to them every week."

"What a noble thing to do," Dex praised. "Despite your situation, you still give to others."

Robert shrugged. "I don't mind helping the Barkers and we get something in return. For that, I'm grateful."

"I'm so sorry about you and your family's misfortune. It's been tough on so many people. Being shapeshifters increases the difficulties. I might have a solution," Dex said.

"My parents own a large property not far from Seattle. They own a hundred acres, much of which is forest. Since my brothers are away at college, my dad could use someone to help maintain the property, clearing downed trees and dead brush. He sells wood chips and compost to local farmers and ships a portion out of state. He has a large unused cabin on the property I'm sure he would allow you and your family to live in. There are schools nearby your kids could attend once in-house school resumes. There's internet in the cabin, so Mikey and Jessica could do school online. I'll give him a call first thing in the morning."

There were tears in Robert's eyes. "Thank you so much for your kindness. It's been a long time since anyone has been so generous."

"It's not a done deal until I speak to my father, but I don't think he would object. He's been looking to hire someone for a while. He would prefer to hire a shapeshifter or were. It's less complicated that way."

Robert put his arm around his wife, who was crying. "You've given us hope. We haven't had that in so long."

"It will work out, I'm sure." Dex stood up. "It's getting late and we should head back to our hotel. We'll come by and see you in the morning after breakfast."

Robert smiled and wiped away his tears. "We look forward to it."

*   *   *

"Of course, I'll hire him," Dex's father replied enthusiastically after hearing their story. "I haven't had much luck finding someone who was like us. The business is getting to be too much for me to handle without your brothers. I'll start getting the cabin ready for them."

"That's great to hear, Dad. We'll let Robert and his family know. Talk to you soon."

Dex grinned as he ended the call. "Dad is eager to hire Robert. With the pandemic, there has been increased demand for wood chips. People are staying home and growing their own vegetables."

"I didn't know there was a demand for it," Felicity said. "I haven't done much gardening."

"Wood chips are used to keep weeds in check in gardens and orchards. They also keep the soil hydrated, thus reducing the need to water frequently."

"I never knew that."

Dex picked up his coat and put it on. "Let's go tell Robert and his family. I told my dad we'd bring them to the house and introduce them and let them get set up in the cabin."

"At least they will have a place to call their own before the holidays."

He nodded in agreement. "We came to Leavenworth for a mini-vacation and ended up helping a shifter family in need. There's no better Christmas gift."

Felicity pulled on her coat and zipped it; her face filled with delight. "Isn't that what the season is all about?"

Charlene Johnson is a multi-published author of paranormal romance and romantic suspense from Sacramento, California. She is introducing a spin-off series, *Circle of the Red Scorpion World* in 2021 and her newest book, *Changing the Rules*, Sterling Wood Series, Book 2, will be released Jan 2021.

Websites:
https://www.charlenejohnsonbooks.com
https://www.circleoftheredscorpion.com
https://www.sterlingwoodseries.com

Books:

Circle of the Red Scorpion Series
  Shattered, Book 1
  Avenged, Book 2
  Dawned, Book 3
  Returned, Book 4
  Awakened, Book 5
Sterling Wood Series
  Homecoming, Book 1 - Book Excellence Award finalist
  Changing the Rules, Book 2 – To be released January 25, 2021
Crimes of Passion Series (multi-author series)
  Blown Away, Book 2 - Literary Titan Silver Award
Anthologies
  Birds of a Feather
  More Birds of a Feather
  Destination-The World Volume One & Volume Two
  'Tis The Season
  All Holidays 2020
  Most Ardently, An Austen-Inspired Christmas Collection

BATTEN DOWN THE HATCHES
NORMA JEAN THORNTON

Batten down the hatches – Christmas time is near
No more ghosts or goblins, black cats, witches, fear

Ready for Thanksgiving, decorations on the door
Turkey's in the freezer, all the rest still at the store

Christmas cards, and wrapping paper, tinsel, trees and strings
These are only just a few, of my least favorite things

Clean the house, decorate, set up every table
Buy or make presents, wrap them all, of this I'm surely able

Make the candy, pies and breads; of course, this makes a mess
Write the letter, mail the cards; are we all ready? ...Yes!

Well, ya thought ya were ...

There'll always be one more thing you wanted,
that you forgot to do
Stop stressing yourself, it'll all be fine; no one'll know, but you

GOD'S EYES AND FUZZY HORSES:
A CHRISTMAS MISCELLANY
JUDITH VAUGHAN

I n the mid-1950s Mother wondered if she would ever have grandchildren to fill the bedrooms of the new ranch house she and Daddy had built on the spot where the view of the peaks was the best.

I grew up on our horse ranch in New Mexico along the streams that flowed from the Sangre de Cristos. It was a mountain climate, and around Christmas, Daddy might snap a snowplow on the little Farmall tractor to clear the snow from the lane that connected the house and barn to the road to Las Vegas, the nearest town.

My memory of the episodes of this miscellany began as a hodgepodge of images. I focused on one, which step by step would link to the next, until the scene blossomed into something of a whole.

When I decided to write about the Christmas party, I remembered the golden peanut. I saw myself painting a plain peanut with glue and immersing it into gold glitter that Mother had bought for other decorations.

Then my brain shrieked at me. Dorothy, my bestie from grade school, was there! Amidst the glitter. I called her that day in 2020, and she remembered, too, locating the craft activity to my Dad's woodshop in the basement. She was still in New Mexico after nearly seventy years. I was in California.

In 1956, Mother and I decided to give a Christmas party for the kids who lived in the villages along the road. Some of their parents had worked for the ranch when the barns and corrals were being constructed, and others had contributed to stringing the mile or more of barbed wire fencing that now delineated its borders. Local women cleaned Mother's house and one occasionally helped when we had guests for dinner. But full-time employment was scarce in the canyon. We assembled a guest list of the Hispanic children of those adults and anyone else they suggested.

Armed only with the name and age of each child, Mother and I went to Gambles, a local store with a mix of furniture and household items. The owners beefed up the toy department before Christmas. We picked out a gift for each guest. It was before the days of heavily marketed fad toys, and I recall our choices were pretty basic. These kids didn't have TV.

Daddy and Lorenzo, the main ranch hand, harvested a fir from the back acreage. It was the largest Christmas tree we'd ever had, and we needed extra decorations. Mother and I shopped at Newberry's, the local five and dime, where she spotted a bargain on plain colored glass balls. She bought several boxes of the ornaments, red, green, gold, and silver. She picked out silver and gold glitter and glue with a nozzle tip; we would decorate them ourselves. I invited my best friend Dorothy from town to join us in the glitter fest. She took little breaks to play the piano, but soon we had lots of decorations to fill the tree and extras for her to take home after she spent the night.

"We need to plan a game," Mother said. "Hmm. What will work with kids of all these ages?"

"Too bad it's not an Easter party. We could have an Easter egg hunt."

"How about a peanut hunt?" said Mother. "That would work, and we can cover one peanut with gold glitter and give a special prize for the kid that finds the golden peanut."

Mother added peanuts to the grocery list, and we worked out the rest of the plans. We embraced cake mixes, then a new product, and made cupcakes for everyone. Little cardboard cups marked with *Standard Dairy* provided the ice cream.

The children arrived, shy but smiling, in pick-ups and older-model cars. Some parents waited in their cars. A mother with a toddler stayed for the party.

I called each child forward for their gifts. The presents

were opened with quiet acceptance. It was a simple party. No one had a Santa outfit. The tree itself was the only decoration in our cavernous, pine-paneled living room with windows picturing the snow-covered peaks to the west.

Then it was time for the peanut hunt. We had hidden the golden peanut once, but decided the spot made it too difficult to find. So we moved it, and put it under the hoop-shaped handle of a little brass bucket that held fire-starter. It was in plain sight.

We started the hunt with the younger children, and then let the rest join in after a few minutes. Soon it seemed time to call it off. The kids had returned to the couch and chairs. But no one had found the golden peanut. The little bucket was the perfect camouflage. We gave hint after hint but no one could see it. A very persistent little boy finally jumped up and found it. The special prize was a dollar bill.

As we served the food, the parents came back to claim their children.

One little girl was named Martha. Twenty years later, I was buying shoes at the Pay Less store in Las Vegas.

The clerk noticed my name. "Oh, that Christmas party at your beautiful house in the canyon...I was there." Her voice was breathy. She touched my hand. "I'm Martha Montano. I used to live in the adobe home along the river near your barn. My father would cross your ranch to farm his forty acres that adjoined yours." The Christmas party flowed back to my mind. Martha and I chatted about our lives that had unfolded since.

Through the winter, I didn't pay much attention to our fifteen horses, a breeding herd of Tennessee walkers. On school days, there was no daylight. During Christmas break, I would give them some basic grooming, teasing burrs out of their manes, and trimming the hair around their faces.

The four stalls in the barn were used for foaling – the other horses spent the winter in the open, in acres of pasture along the Gallinas, officially a river, but in winter a narrow sparkling mountain stream, never completely freezing, but edged with the rime of ice for much of December. We fed the horses hay twice a day, and they drank at will from the river. When it snowed, they sheltered together as a cozy herd among the cottonwoods.

I rode less than I did in the summer, but when I did, it was bareback, my legs and buttocks cushioned and warmed by the extravagant winter coats of my favorites, Babe and Dash. I loved crossing the stream, its melody the tinkle of the water flowing in and out of the ice.

Years later, my mother welcomed her grown daughters home for Christmas with their families. In 1972 I made Gods Eyes out of yarn with my sister Mary and her three young daughters. We hung a spreading pine bough over the fireplace and placed the colorful squares of wound yarn on it. No tree that year. After we admired our arty creation, we gathered in the hall, light reflected from an antique mirror. We sang every Christmas carol we knew. My daughter Betsy was two and Mary's girls were in elementary school.

I'd never seen Mother so happy. This is the last Christmas I remember in any detail. The ranch was sold in 1978.

Judith Vaughan grew up in Northern New Mexico engrossed in her father's horse breeding hobby. She left the family ranch for boarding school in Colorado and then attended Carleton College and the University of New Mexico School of Medicine. She has composed stories since childhood, and began to hone the craft of writing after forty years practicing medicine. She lives in Elk Grove, California, and writes with Elk Grove Writers and Artists. Works in progress include her New Mexico memoir, *Strawberry Roan*. Her stories have placed in short story contests and have been published in NCPA Anthologies.

She is a member of the California Writers Club, Northern California Publishers and Authors, and the New Mexico Book Association.

Contact her at jfbvaughan@comcast.net.

MIXING METAPHORS
SUSAN BETH FURST

A Christmas/Hannukah Haibun (a haibun is a prose poem combined with a haiku):

Hanukkah Claus slides down the chimney, eats the Christmas cookies I left for him, and leaves me some latkes on the empty plate. He fills the stockings with dreidels and gelt before flying back to the North Pole on his magic menorah.

Merry Hanumas! Happy Chrismukkah! And to all a good night!

Holidaze…
too much Mogen David
in the fruitcake

*   *   *

HAIKU
Eight haiku total in the categories of Halloween, Valentine's Day, Advent, and Christmas.

Halloween - 1

Trick or Treat
the littlest ghost
wags his tail

Valentine's Day - 1

the hopeful barista
puts his heart in a mug

she breaks it

Advent - 1

advent calendar
the last piece of chocolate
melts in my mouth

Christmas – 5

Christmas in Japan I trim the bonsai

hoar frost
the old horse
jingles his bells

midnight mass—
the shepherds asleep
in the back seat

first noel
even the moon
wears a halo

porcelain doll
she crosses the border
to Toyland

*   *   *

Definitions of a few of the different types Japanese poetry mentioned

Haiku is a three-line, beautifully descriptive, form of poetry, intended to be read in one breath. If read in Japanese, most traditional haiku would have five syllables, or sounds, in the first line, seven in the second, and five in the last. The Academy of American Poets asserts, "As the form evolved, many of these rules - including the 5-7-5 practice - have routinely been broken…"

Haibun (literally, **haikai** writings) is a prosimetric (Written partly in prose and partly in verse) literary form originating in Japan, combining prose and haiku. The range of **haibun** is broad and frequently includes autobiography, diary, essay, prose poem, short story and travel journal.

Haikai - Wikipedia
https://en.wikipedia.org/wiki/Haikai
Haikai (Japanese comic, unorthodox) a popular genre of Japanese linked verse, which developed in the sixteenth century out of the earlier aristocratic **renga.** "Haikai" may also refer to other poetic forms that embrace the haikai aesthetic, including haiku

Renga - Wikipedia
https://en.wikipedia.org/wiki/Renga
Japanese linked poetry in the form of a **tanka** (or series of tanka), with the first three lines composed by one person and the second two by another. A typical renga sequence is comprised of 100 stanzas composed by about three poets in a single sitting.

Tanka is a Japanese poem consisting of 31 syllables in five lines of 5, 7, 5, 7, 7 syllables, and generally **do not rhyme.**

Susan Beth Furst is a Touchstone Award nominated Japanese short-form poet and Children's picture book author. She's published three haiku collections: Souvenir Shop: Memories of the Highland Park Zoo, Road to Utopia, and Neon Snow. She also writes haibun, and "57" was chosen to appear in Old Song: The Red Moon Anthology of English-Language Haiku (2017). Susan's books for children include Humpty Dumpty Cracks and All, Electric Pink: A Christmas Haibun, and The Amazing Glass House: A Haiku Storybook. The Hole In My Haiku is now available (October, 2020). Susan lives in Fishersville, Virginia, with her husband Herb and a canary named Mozart.

You can find Susan at PaperWhistlePress.com and on Instagram @susanbethfurstpoet..

ONE CHRISTMAS NIGHT
ELAINE FABER

One Christmas night, you entered on tiny cat paws
Even though we didn't need another cat.
Uninvited! Unasked! Unthinkable!

Our routine changed that day. Catnip mice.
One more mouth to feed!
Irrelevant! Immaterial! Unimportant!

Plastic balls and shredded paper litter the floor
The old cats reel! Who invited this stranger?
Chaos! Confusion! Cacophony!

As suddenly as you came…you were gone - the silent killer
You carried inside, prevailed.
A void now impossible to fill
Sadness - Sorrow - Silence.

Mama, please go to Heaven's gate.
There's a tiny kitty waiting there.
I know you'll love each other.
Mischievous - Inquisitive- Adorable!

HOLIDAY INTERRUPTED

LAURA ROBERTS

It just figures. As soon as we get on the road headed south, there's a big mess on the freeway. A couple of tractor trailers managed to jackknife on the highway, causing a huge crash and blocking off traffic on the only route out of this frozen wasteland of a city. Awesome. Great work, truckers. How does someone jackknife a semi, anyway? What, exactly, does it take to qualify as "jackknifing"?

I ask Dr. Google, and he informs me many accidents, such as this one, occur because of improper brake maintenance or adjustment. To "jackknife" a truck means the cab has skidded in one direction, whilst the trailer has headed in the opposite direction. Indeed, many of these types of crashes involve trucks flipping over completely, due to being entirely out of control. Thanks, doc.

After about fifteen minutes of inching forward in stop-and-go traffic, I finally spot the exit for the overpass oasis and pull the car over to the shoulder so we can access the ramp. The parking lot is close to overflowing, but I manage to find a free space near the gas station. We head inside and go straight to the enormous overpass windows to get a bird's-eye view of the scene. Looking down at the traffic that's backed up for miles, it's clear we're marooned here for the time being. On the plus side, we can stretch our legs inside this restaurant-slash-rest-area while we wait for the mess to get cleaned up, but we're still stuck on this highway for the foreseeable future.

"All I ever wanted in this world was a nice Christmas vacation," Anna groans.

"And I was the idiot who thought he was gonna give it to you," I grumble in frustrated solidarity.

"It's not your fault," she replies, and kisses me on the

cheek.

"No, but I *did* try to suggest an earlier departure time," I remind her.

"You know I can't miss my stories." She leans her head on my shoulder, still pondering the frosty mess on the freeway.

"*This* is a story," I say, gesturing with my left arm.

"Some story. We started down to Florida for a Christmas getaway, and five minutes into the drive we had to pull off at a rest stop because the highway's closed on the Dan Ryan all the way down to Champaign."

"The Dan Ryan doesn't go to Champaign," I point out.

"You know what I mean," she says, raising her head so she can punch my shoulder.

"Anyway," I say, rubbing my shoulder where she's socked me, "my point is that this trip is ruined, and in related news, Christmas is canceled, too."

"Don't be a Grinch. Christmas isn't canceled just because we can't make it to Florida," she corrects me.

"Well, Florida *was* the totality of my gift to you this year…"

"But holidays don't just *not happen* because you're not where you wanted to be. Think of all the people who get stuck in airports. And bus stations. And who can't even afford to travel to see their family for the holidays."

"I guess you have a point," I begrudgingly agree. I do actually have another gift for her, and it would've been a lot nicer to give it in Florida, but she's right. You can pull a ring out of your pocket just about anywhere, if the moment feels appropriately romantic. Can't you? Probably not in a noisy, crowded, mud brown and mustard yellow, crusty, rusty rest area, though. Even Anna, who loves to tell me to "turn that frown upside down," would agree that our current surroundings leave a lot to be desired in terms of ambiance.

"Hang on, I got an idea. Wait here." She pulls away, makes a little square with her fingers like she's taking my picture through an old-timey camera, and then scurries off down the brown-tiled hallway, leaving me alone in this glassed-in limbo full of lost souls wandering the corridor between the north and southbound sides of the highway.

Where the hell is she going to go? There's nowhere *to* go, unless you count the McDonald's, where the line's backed up about as far as the expressway, full of angry drivers who think some special sauce and a Reindeer Treat is gonna cure what ails them. I don't even want to think about the line-up at the restrooms.

I puff out my breath on the overpass window and it leaves a fog against the cold glass. I idly draw a heart with the initials "JQ + AV" in it, then scrawl "4EVA" underneath. What am I, twelve? I know, it's cheesy, right? But I can't help myself. Anna's the whole reason we're on this doomed holiday trip. Me, I'm content to stay here in the frozen city, eking out a living doing whatever odd jobs I can find until the New Year thaw. But she wants more. Tropical island vacation more. Florida's about as close as we could get, on our budget, especially since being able to drive there is the key to keeping costs down. It's a 20-hour drive, one-way (minus delays for snow and *jackknifed semis*, thank you very much), but it'll all be worth it to see her smile. Preferably in one of those itsy-bitsy teeny-weenie bikinis she's got stuffed in her bag.

Sun, sand, sex. That's why people go to Florida in the middle of winter, right? Maybe to drink a couple of tropical beverages on the beach? Maybe for some theme park thrills, if they can swing it? We can't afford any magical mice, but a couple of mojitos are definitely on the menu.

I pass my sleeve over the heart with our initials so I can clear the fog.

Anna returns, walking towards me with something hidden behind her back.

"That better not be from the golden arches," I warn.

She just giggles. "Close your eyes."

"I'm not opening my mouth."

"Close 'em!"

I close my eyes. I feel her take my hand and put something soft and furry into it. "What the...?"

Opening my eyes, I see a pint-sized purple llama.

Before I can ask, she shouts: "Merry Christmas! It's a

loot llama. I won him in the grabber machine by the entrance."

I raise an eyebrow, confused.

"He's good luck. Or, anyway, he's supposed to bring you loot. Cash money. Gold ducats. Cheddar. Clams. Cold hard cash. Get it?"

I laugh. "Not entirely, but I like your enthusiasm, kid." I kiss her on the forehead. "Thanks."

"Do you think we'll get out of here tonight?" she asks, snuggling back against my shoulder as we stand there looking at the line of backed-up cars. The sun is sinking lower in the sky, giving the scene a strangely beautiful glow amidst the swirling snowflakes.

"Ain't nobody getting outta here tonight," an older man in a MAGA hat proclaims. I'm not sure how long he's been standing there, about six feet away from us, staring out at the highway, but he takes a long sip from a tallboy of Budweiser that's barely hidden in a paper sack after prognosticating.

"How do you know?" Anna asks him.

"Radio says there's six more inches of snow on the way. Even if they clear out them semis, ain't nobody gonna be able to plow with all these cars parked on the road."

"Dammit."

"Maybe we'll get lucky," Anna says, patting the purple llama. "It could be a pre-Christmas miracle."

"Maybe," I say, hoping for the best, but assuming the worst.

"Not a chance in hell," MAGA-hat says. "So much for global warming."

"That's... not how global warming works," I mutter under my breath.

"Thanks for the info," Anna says, leading me away from the window and towards some overflow seating outside the McDonald's.

"What, you didn't want me to get into a fistfight with a climate change denier?" I joke when he's out of earshot.

She just gives me a look as we plunk down in a tiny booth built for two, that had suddenly become vacant. I place the llama on the table next to the plastic salt and pepper shakers.

"So, what's the plan?" she asks me.

"I don't think there *is* a plan," I say. "Basically, we're stuck here until further notice. That could be two hours or two days, for all we know."

We both sigh in defeat. I try not to think about the pre-paid hotel room.

"We'll get to Florida eventually, babe, I swear."

She smiles weakly, but I can see the tears shining in her eyes.

"Come on. Let's go take a nap in the car. Everything will feel better after we get some rest, right?"

"Won't we freeze to death out there?"

"I've got a full tank of gas and a Spotify playlist long enough to take us to Jupiter."

"There'd better be some Prince on that playlist," she says with a suggestive grin.

We exit the rest area and retire to the backseat of my beat-up Honda, crank "Darling Nikki," fog up the windows, and fall asleep in each other's arms.

After what could be several hours or several days, we wake up to a raging storm of cars honking, all in different patterns and at slightly different tones – a symphony of cacophony. At first it sounds like a thousand angry New Yorkers are trying to urge an elderly woman to get the hell out of the crosswalk, but after I rub the sleep from my eyes, I realize this is actually a happy sound. A *very* happy sound, indeed.

To my left, the highway is backed up with honking cars. To my right, the highway is utterly clear and pristine, for perhaps the first time in decades.

Back on the left, the cars that are honking are attempting to wake up all the drivers sleeping in the cars parked at what is now the front of the line to continue forward on the empty highway. One by one, drivers are waking up to the sound of car horns blaring, blearily starting up their engines, and driving off slowly, as if they might still be dreaming.

The llama worked! It's a pre-Christmas miracle!

Anna and I grab our lucky charm from the dashboard, each give him a kiss, give one another a quick kiss, and then race to see who can get all their clothes back on first.

Florida – warm, exotic Florida, completely devoid of snow, the future site of all my happiest holiday memories – awaits.

 Laura Roberts writes travel themed contemporary romance, with her steamy stories under the pen name Laure L'Amour.

Dabbling in both factual and fictional genres, Laura has penned 27 books for adults, including the alphabetical travel guides *Montreal From A to Z* and *San Diego From A to Z,* offbeat writing guides *NaNoWriMo: A Cheater's Guide* and *Confessions of a 3-Day Novelist,* a collection of capital city meet-cutes called *Sacramento Love,* as well as three nonfiction career guides for young adults *(Careers in Gaming, Careers If You Like Music,* and *Careers in Digital Media)* published by ReferencePoint Press. She currently lives in Sacramento with her artist husband and their literary kitties, and can be found online at Buttontapper.com.

AROUND THE TINSEL PINE

DENISE LEE BRANCO

A red glass Santa, which topped its towering peak, aluminum foil needles affixed to silver branches that extended from its trunk, and a spinning wheel's illumination of green, red, orange and blue hues that shone upon the aluminum Christmas tree from floor level, may be considered vintage by today's standards, but to me it represents timeless joy.

While many families, outfitted in their hooded coats and winter gloves drove miles to Christmas tree farms to choose the most fragrant, freshest Douglas fir, slugged it to their car and strapped it to the rooftop for the ride home, mine didn't have to go far. Our tradition began at our family living room window near the wood stove. There we ate popcorn, hoping to save enough for stringing garland, discussed what we wanted Santa to bring us, and created an indoor festive holiday masterpiece from the floor up, while in our pajamas.

My newlywed parents purchased an artificial Christmas tree from the Sears & Roebuck Christmas Catalog in 1962 because of the alluring easy payment plan. It was their gift to each other and to the family they were starting. Owning an aluminum Christmas tree and its rotating four-color wheel was economical, especially for young families like ours who lived on a budget and didn't have spare money to buy real trees every year.

Our tree-decorating tradition involved the whole family, including our dog, Susie. My dad would pull a three-foot box from behind hanging clothes at the back of my parents' bedroom closet and bring it to our annual project location. He'd piece together the trunk until it rose to its six-foot height and then place it in an aluminum stand. Mom would remove individually-wrapped branches from the box and categorize each of them according to their tiny color-coded dots, spreading groups across the low-pile carpeting. I'd take a branch, match the color-coded dot at its tip to the same one on a one-eighth-inch round opening in the aluminum tree trunk, and insert. Branches were of different lengths, which required attention to detail in order to meet the triangular-shaped goal.

Susie, of Pekingese/Dachshund blended perfection, lived up to her breed's reputation for loyalty. I never felt like an only child with Susie always at my side. She was six months older than me, and was my devoted best friend. Every Christmas, Susie, donned in her green, red, and white knit sweater, sat next to me by the tree as I opened presents. She knew her patient presence would eventually lead to personal bliss.

After everyone opened their gifts on Christmas morning each year, I'd walk over to the red felt stocking inscribed with Susie's name in silver glitter and glue, tacked above the colorful faux andirons and flickering flames of our Sears & Roebuck Christmas Catalog's cardboard brick fireplace, as Susie closely followed. I'd pull out a wrapped rectangular-shaped reward and show it to her at nose level; she'd smell it and tail-wagging ensued.

While I ripped off the outer gift wrap as quick as kids do, Susie wiggled faster. The look of heavenly delight on her face was priceless when she first saw the unveiled brown wrapper. It was a full-size Hershey's milk chocolate bar. Back in those days, we had no idea chocolate was toxic to dogs. Nevertheless, that edible gift was the highlight of Susie's first Christmas, and for fifteen happy years thereafter.

As a kid, I was obsessed with putting puzzles together. Hanging ornaments and garland on a Christmas tree is a cheery pastime many of us enjoy, but building an artificial tree one piece at a time, for an avid puzzle fan like me, was way more fun. I remember my excitement when I could insert branches higher up the tree because I had grown taller than I was the previous Christmas.

When I was four years old, sitting on the floor beside the Christmas tree with my parents watching from our couch, I opened a gift which symbolized my father's pride as a volunteer firefighter in our community. I sat perplexed at how to operate the brick-red fire engine with its elongated white ladder. Dad knelt beside me and pointed out the features of my (and his) new toy. He turned the fire engine on and it lurched forward, sirens blaring, red lights flashing. I scrammed, crying in fear for my life, never to return to the scene of the "fire". Sorry, Dad.

Roller-skating reemerged as a trendy activity during the 1970s disco era. Birthday parties at my hometown roller rink were gaining in popularity during my childhood and I wanted to be prepared for an invitation. A pair of roller skates was the number one request on my Christmas wish list when I was seven.

That wish became reality on Christmas morning when I pulled a holiday-wrapped square box from underneath our tree, tore it open with eager anticipation, and pulled out my future—a brand-new pair of skates! They were made of two separate pieces of metal which collapsed and expanded for growing feet and chosen shoe type. A metal key locked in the proper fit and an attached leather strap kept the skates in place. I was ever so grateful for my parents' gift made possible by, you guessed it, Sears & Roebuck Christmas Catalog's easy payment plan.

Skating in my metal roller-skates on the gravel driveway entrance to our ranch was a clunky endeavor. I was in for a halting surprise if a skate wasn't adequately tightened. I'd give it my all but the sheer energy involved would sideline my overly optimistic efforts in a few short minutes. The best alternative was a long, but narrow concrete pathway from the driveway to the house. It would hold me over until the weekend when I could visit my *Ava* (the Portuguese language term for grandmother) in town.

A concrete slab ran the full length of Ava's house from corner to corner in the back, next to the lawn. It connected to another concrete section which spread across the front of the detached two-car garage and three-foot sidewalks that bordered her house. Ava's property was a skater's paradise. I spent countless hours in her backyard testing my skills at staying upright by varying speeds, turning in circles, and skating backwards. I could have skated from dawn to dusk if allowed. My new roller skates were my all-time favorite present under the tree that year.

We can't physically return to our childhood Christmases, but memories are eternal. It's those holiday moments with family that we cherish the most. Though those years are long gone, our family's reliable Tinsel Pine will always have a special place in my heart along with two loving parents, a loyal fur-sibling, a Portuguese grandmother...and the Sears & Roebuck Christmas Catalog.

 Denise Lee Branco is an award-winning author and inspirational speaker, who continues to believe, dream, and overcome so those who meet her recognize the possibilities within them. Denise's first book, *Horse at the Corner Post: Our Divine Journey*, won a silver medal in the Living Now Book Awards.

Denise is a longtime member of Northern California Publishers and Authors and a current member of several other writing and publishing organizations. She has been a contributor to multiple anthologies.

Denise is currently working on her next book *The Ride to Purpose: Finding Freedom on the Trail of Life*. She lives in the foothills of Northern California and loves biking on nature trails, foods with melted cheese, and spoiling her three rescues.

Visit www.DeniseInspiresYou.com to learn more.

A PERFECT DAY
SUSAN BETH FURST

It is a warm day for November. The sun is shining, and white clouds hang as if suspended in the blue sky. The air is crisp and tart. Pots of yellow spider mums line the steps leading up to my mother's house. The front door is open, and the large beveled glass mirror in the hall reflects the autumn sun. It is a perfect day.

Angelus
a congregation of sparrows
circle the bell tower

Mom is in the kitchen, basting, drippings sizzle as she overshoots the turkey. Eugene is placing a bet with the neighborhood bookie. GG is on her perch drinking Pepsi as Joshua toddles from the candy dish to the chair, leaving chocolate smudges on her new favorite purse. My pumpkin pies are on the buffet. They are warm and fragrant, and there is nary a crack in the speckled orange-glossy filling. It is a perfect day.

centerpiece
the old pilgrim
missing a buckle

The table is loaded to the point of sagging with turkey, stuffing, sweet potato casserole, and GG's special canned-shrimp cocktail. I smile to myself as I reach for my pies, my Better Homes and Garden's perfect pies. But my joy turns to horror as I see two large craters where the orange-glossy filling used to be. I look at my laughing son and grab the Reddi-Wip. I give it a shake, press my finger against the nozzle, and proceed to smother the tops of my pies. It is a perfect day.

sticky fingers
covering up
the family secrets

A NATIONAL DAY FOR EVERYONE

BOB IRELAN

Everyone has one or two favorite holidays. Mine are Christmas and Thanksgiving because of what they mean and because they always include family gatherings. They are among the ten so-called Federal Holidays.

Ah, but each year offers so much more. In addition to a number of other well-known holidays, almost every day of the year is a "National Day" that recognizes something ... not really a holiday but, for some, a cause for celebration or, at least, recognition. More than a few of these National Days pay tribute to a food or drink (like Sloppy Joe Day on March 18 or Pina Colada Day on July 10), but the list extends far beyond that.

An abbreviated month-by-month examination of National Days provides the following essential reminders:

January offers some of my personal favorites. National Bobblehead Day on the 7th is followed by National Nothing Day on the 16th, and National Opposite Day on the 25th precedes National Kazoo Day on the 28th.

February includes the ever-popular National Shower with a Friend Day on the 5th and the National Random Acts of Kindness Day on the 17th. National Love Your Pet Day and National Sticky Bun Day occur one after the other on the 20th and 21st.

Not to be outdone, March opens up on the 1st with National Dadgum That's Good Day, followed by National Old Stuff Day on the 2nd, National Panic Day one week later, and National Goof Off Day (I've noted this one in red on my calendar) on the 22nd.

April Fool's month includes, thank goodness, National Beer Day on the 7th along with National Bean Counter Day on the 16th and, very importantly, National Zipper Day on the 29th.

Moving on to May, we have National Lost Sock Memorial Day on the 9th, appropriately followed the next day by National Clean Up Your Room Day and, here's one you'll want to be sure to note, National Dance Like a Chicken Day on the 14th.

June leaps out of the chute on the 1st with National Go Barefoot Day, followed the next day by National Rocky Road Day, and, on the 3rd, by National Insect Repellant Awareness Day (don't say I didn't warn you).

July's Independence Day immediately follows National Eat Your Beans Day on the 3rd. Later in the month, the 14th is National Nude Day and the 21st is National Junk Food Day.

Poor August has no Federal holiday but it compensates for that omission by offering National Underwear Day on the 5th, National Happiness Happens Day on the 8th, and National Bad Poetry Day on the 18th.

September starts with National No Rhyme (Nor Reason) Day on the 1st and proceeds to National Ampersand Day on the 8th and the much-ignored but desperately-needed National Punctuation Day on the 24th.

One has to wait till October for the National Be Bald and Be Free Day (the 14th), National Suspenders Day on the 20th, and National Greasy Food Day on the 25th. These three are enough to make October "my month."

Sharing November with Thanksgiving is National Fancy Rat & Mouse Day (what?) on the 12th, National Occult Day on the 18th, and National Pins & Needles Day on the 27th.

Okay, dear reader, we're almost done. Among the lesser-known December "days" are National Bathtub Party Day (the 5th), National Ding-A-Ling Day on the 12th, and, of course, National Wear Your Pearls Day on the 15th.

As indicated earlier, this is only a partial listing. But care has been taken to provide the essentials. You're welcome.

 Following 10 years of newspaper and magazine reporting and editing, including stints at The Wall Street Journal and Nation's Business magazine in Washington, DC, Bob Irelan spent 32 years managing public relations for a Fortune 500 family of companies.

In retirement, he taught a public relations course for two years at University of the Pacific and for five years at University of California, Davis, Extension.

He is the author of two novels. The first, *Angel's Truth -- One teenager's quest for justice*, was published in 2018 and took second place in Fiction at NCPA's 25th Annual Book Awards. The second, *Justifiable -- Murder in the Mountain State,* was published in September 2020.

Bob's short stories are among those included in these NCPA anthologies: *Birds of a Feather, More Birds of a Feather*, and *Destination: The World, Volumes One, & Two* He lives in Rancho Murieta, California.

MOM'S SILVERWARE
ELAINE FABER

Corrine sighed as the comforting scent of turkey wafted through the dining room. She glanced at the clock, mentally judging her dinner's progress with the anticipated arrival of the children. Her mother's china, crystal wine goblets and silverware were lovingly arranged on the dining room table. She continued polishing a silver fork from her mother's rosewood silverware box and placed it next to a wine goblet.

She remembered the holidays at Mom's house when all the grandchildren came to dinner. The lights from her chandelier had shimmered and bounced off each shining goblet and piece of silverware. Mom would move a spoon a fraction of an inch until it was just right and then, placed a chocolate kiss on each plate.

"There," she would say, "that's so they know they are loved."

Corrine's husband mumbled something unintelligible from the family room. "What are you doing in there?" Corrine called.

"I'm converting your Dad's old 8- mm movie films to VHS. We can show the grandkids pictures from your childhood."

Corrine returned to the kitchen and poured herself a glass of wine. She pulled her mother's casserole dish from the cupboard. Her thoughts turned again to memories of past holidays.

She recalled the Christmases and Thanksgivings when Mom and "the girls" all bought party dresses specifically for the event. The tradition ended when her mother passed away.

Through the years, Corrine moved up a generation in the family chain. She had become the gray haired "Grandma," and her daughter took her place. Different little children bustled through the house.

Where have the years gone? she thought.

Corrine returned to the dining room and placed the polished fork on the table. Mom's silverware was a tradition that had been present for 60 years, throughout years of young motherhood and still remained a part of every holiday dinner. It was a constant, defying the loss of loved ones, gray hair, or climbing through the links of the family chain. The silverware would grace her daughter's table some day; a reminder of her childhood holiday memories. It would become part of her tradition as she created new memories with her children.

Where did Mom get the silverware? It was not likely to have been a wedding present. Mom and Dad were married during the Great Depression.

Corrine admired her table setting. It looked nice. "Oh! I almost forget the kiss!" she said, adding Mom's droplets of chocolate love on each plate.

Mom would be pleased.

Her husband interrupted her memories. "Honey, come take a look at this. It's one of your dad's old Christmas movies when you were a baby."

They sat together on the couch, sipping wine, watching the jumpy speckley black and white film flicker across the bed sheet pinned to the wall.

The speckles became Corrine's mother and dad. It was Christmas Day, 1946. Cousins Dolly and Beverly hugged giant dolls and little Allan sat on the floor in front of the Christmas tree. Corrine saw herself, a three-year-old, holding an enormous doll. Her unbelievably young mother smiled from the bed sheet. Corrine's nine-year-old brother chased little cousin Allan around the room with his new BB gun, making faces at the camera. Big sister and Cousin Wilbur ripped open puzzles and books. Only one last gift remained.

Dad handed a large package to Mom. She smiled,

looking uncomfortable in the spotlight. The Christmas wrap fell away. She opened the beautiful rosewood box filled with shiny new silverware. Her face beamed and she mouthed a silent "thank you."

How Dad must have sacrificed to buy such an expensive gift in 1946 when jobs were scarce and times were hard.

Here was the birth of Corrine's most precious family tradition; the beautiful rosewood box filled with silverware. A connection she still shared with her mother, one that she would continue to share with her daughter and her granddaughter for years to come.

The oven buzzer sounded. The turkey was done. Corrine wiped the tears from her eyes, picked up her wine goblet and hurried to the kitchen. Time was getting away and the children would soon be here!

Elaine Faber lives in Northern California with her husband and feline companions. She is a member of Sisters in Crime, Cat Writers Association, and Northern California Publishers and Authors. Her short stories have appeared in national magazines, won multiple awards in various contests, and are featured in multiple anthologies. She leads a critique group in the Sacramento area.

Elaine's novels have won top awards from the 2017, 2018, and 2019 Northern California Publishers and Authors annual contests, and Certificates of Excellence from the 2018 and 2019 Cat Writers' Association.

Elaine is currently working on three fiction novels to be published next year.

http://tinyurl.com/lrvevgm — Black Cat's Legacy

http://tinyurl.com/lg7yvgq — Black Cat and the Lethal Lawyer

http://tinyurl.com/07zcsm2 — Black Cat and the Accidental Angel

http://tinyurl.com/vgyp89s — Black Cat and the Secret in Dewey's Diary

http://tinyrul.com/hdbvzsv — Mrs. Odboddy – Hometown Patriot

http://tinyurl.com/jn5bzwb — Mrs. Odboddy Undercover Courier

http://tinyrulcoom/yx72fcpx — Mrs. Odboddy And Then There was a Tiger

GRATEFUL SENSES

JACKIE ALCALDE MARR

The flutter of red, rust, and gold
The china glistening in candle glow
The extra table and folding chairs
The gourds with bumps and colored corn
Thankful for the sights

Smoke from logs and ember glow
Onion and celery and pungent garlic
Sweet yeast and sage and savory thyme
Apples and cinnamon, pumpkin, and cloves
Thankful for the scents

Chatter and laughter and cheers of a touchdown
Clank of ice cubes and clink of the glass
Thunderous feet of children on hard wood
Stories of family from long, long ago
Thankful for the sounds

Salty peanuts and rippled chips
A generous foul, succulent and moist
The burst of butter on pillows of mash
Dry tongue and tobacco from a big Cabernet
Thankful for the tastes

Grandma's fragile hand in yours
A kiss on your cheek, cold face rescued from the wind
The tightest embrace from a year that's passed
The strong grip of the infant's fingers
Thankful for the touch

Let us give thanks

DAYS WAY OFF
STEVE PASTIS

The Carolers

They were a festively dressed bunch with lots of scarves and woolen caps. Greens and reds abounded.

They rang the bell at the home of Henrietta and Mr. Bleepers on a cold evening in early winter and started singing before the front door opened. They sang a song of peace and goodwill, but Henrietta, the co-homeowner who opened the door, didn't recognize any of the songs they sang.

There were no Christmas trees or mangers or Figgy pudding mentioned in any of their songs.

"What kind of Christmas songs are those?" asked Henrietta with some measure of disgust in her voice.

"They aren't Christmas songs," said Mattie, a large round woman with large round glasses. "We're atheists."

"Why are you caroling?" asked Henrietta.

"We like the idea of singing to our neighbors as winter begins."

"Isn't that a Christmas tradition?"

"Well, we like it anyway — even if we are atheists."

"Would you like cookies — even if they are shaped like Christmas trees?"

"Yes, we have no problem with trees. We know they exist. We can see them."

Henrietta went to the dining room and brought out a large tray of Christmas tree cookies. Each caroler took one.

Henrietta pointed above Mattie's head. "Do you know what that is?" Henrietta asked.

"Yes, mistletoe," Mattie replied and grabbed Arthur, the tall skinny fellow next to her, and kissed him. Arthur seemed

110

startled, but he was also smiling and blushing.

"Is that another Christmas tradition you're okay with?"

"Yes, we have no problem with kisses. We know they exist."

With that, the carolers left to serenade the next house. Henrietta sat back in her easy chair.

"What was all that about?" asked Mr. Bleepers.

"I think that was a small skirmish in the war on Christmas," said Henrietta, looking puzzled. "I'm just not sure which side won."

Pachyderm Christmas

"It's a Pachyderm Christmas!" announced Uncle Blotto from the evil neighbors' balcony.

"It's a Pachyderm Christmas!" he shouted a few minutes later from the roof of the old Baxter house across the street.

Aunt Zenith gave him two points for each proclamation. She kept score on a large chalkboard that rested on a folding chair in their living room.

"It's an Etruscan Yuletide!" shouted Mr. Bleepers from the top of the telephone pole on the corner.

"He gets one point for that," said Aunt Zenith.

"Only one point?" I inquired. "Why not two points like Uncle Blotto?"

"He didn't have to trespass to proclaim," she explained.

"I think that technically Mr. Bleepers is trespassing," I said. "The telephone pole is the property of the telephone company."

"But they don't use poison blow darts like our evil neighbors, or own a Kodiak bear like the people who moved into the old Baxter place."

I was quiet. Uncle Blotto wasn't.

"It's a Pachyderm Christmas!" he shouted while hang gliding over the neighborhood.

"That's three points," said Aunt Zenith. "Your uncle is terrified of acrobats."

"It's an Etruscan Yuletide!" yelled Mr. Bleepers while

111

suspended by his feet from a rope ladder hanging from a helicopter that was circling the neighborhood.

"Two points," said Aunt Zenith. I didn't ask why.

"It's a Tyrannosaurus Noel!" shouted a round bespectacled fellow with a bullet-shaped helmet as he flew past our front door en route from a cannon.

"Who is he?" I asked.

"I don't really know," replied Aunt Zenith. "He's not one of the regulars on the circuit. He must be an amateur looking to break into the competition."

"No points?" I asked.

"No points," replied Aunt Zenith.

Uncle Blotto ran through the front doorway, through the house, and into the back room, which served as his headquarters for reasons never explained to me. A few minutes later, he emerged wearing a shiny silver jumpsuit and a shiny copper-colored helmet.

"Tell them I meant well," he told us. He kissed Aunt Zenith on the cheek and dashed back outside.

A moment later, the living room darkened and Aunt Zenith and I went outside to see what happened to the afternoon sunshine. A large blimp was hovering over the houses across the street. We could see Mr. Bleepers with the pilot in the blimp's gondola. As soon as he saw us, he gave a thumbs-up sign.

Suddenly, there was a light show on the side of the blimp. Animation replaced the random lights and we saw several cartoon Etruscans sitting around a Christmas tree. The cartoon faded and the words "It's an Etruscan Yuletide!" appeared. The words changed colors a few times before giving way to the words "Nyeah! Nyeah! Nyeah!"

Aunt Zenith was crestfallen. She erased the score from the chalkboard and put it into the entry closet. The game was clearly over and Mr. Bleepers had won.

We wondered if Uncle Blotto knew the game was over, until we saw him an hour later, running down the street in his shiny silver jumpsuit and shiny copper-colored helmet. He was shouting something, but we couldn't understand what he was saying at first because he was five or six houses away.

"It's a Mercurial Pentecost!" he shouted as he passed by us.

Mr. Bleepers had been standing across the street awaiting his hard-earned accolades until the moment Uncle Blotto passed by him. Mr. Bleepers had spent all his money, energy and inspiration on his blimp effort and knew he didn't have the resources to compete with Uncle Blotto's simple change in tactics. It was Mr. Bleepers' turn to be crestfallen.

When Uncle Blotto returned home, Aunt Zenith welcomed him as a conquering hero. He truly understood the secret to being a winner.

If at first you don't succeed, change the game.

A Smattering of Yellow

Ed wore a white shirt with a smattering of yellow to his city's Arbor Day parade in hopes of catching the attention of vivacious Yolanda.

"Hey, nice smattering of yellow," said Doris the librarian, who was suddenly in his path.

"Thank you," mumbled Ed.

"Just a thank you?" asked Doris. "I guess it's not your fault that you don't see an opportunity when it's standing right in front of you."

"And I guess it's not your fault that you aren't vivacious," replied Ed, effectively ending the conversation and allowing him to search the crowd for vivacious Yolanda.

Ed finally met up with Yolanda in front of the abandoned stationery building. She stood arm-in-arm with Vic, a towering fellow who wore a bright yellow shirt.

"Hello Yolanda," said Ed.

"Beat it, smatter boy," replied Yolanda. "I'm here with Vic and he isn't shy about wearing a shirt that is completely yellow."

"Yes, beat it, smatter boy," echoed Vic.

As Ed walked away, the Arbor Day parade started and representatives of several civic groups passed by carrying trees. People festively threw acorns in their direction.

"This has the makings of the worst Arbor Day ever," thought Ed.

Not paying attention to anything but the stray acorn he kicked down the sidewalk, Ed bumped into a local cashier named Clara. She was vivacious and her blouse was a bright shade of yellow.

"This could be the start of the best Arbor Day ever," thought Ed until he saw the crowbar in her hand and the angry look in her eyes.

"Out of the way, smatter boy," said Clara. "Some hussy is messing with my Vic."

Ed decided to buy two bottles of Dr Pepper and some Corn Nuts and watch all the national Arbor Day festivities on television. He also decided to change his shirt.

"At least this Arbor Day is much better than last year's," he thought. "I chatted with three women and two of them were vivacious."

Pentecost Sunday

The Andrews kid came by as I was getting my Sunday paper out of the azalea bed. He was all dressed up for church and wanted me to notice the new tie his mother had bought him for Pentecost Sunday. I pretended to share his enthusiasm. I was nice and polite, and I didn't ask him if his tie glowed in the dark.

When I got back inside, I poured a cup of coffee and turned on the local morning news. The lead story was about a leopard that had escaped from the city zoo. They showed a photo of the leopard above the phone number for someone to call if they saw it. I probably would have called, even if the leopard I saw was a different one.

Edgar, of "calling for no apparent reason" fame, called during the sports news. Whatever he said, I politely listened to – or at least I was quiet at the right times. He didn't seem to notice when I set the phone down to go and pour myself more coffee. Fortunately, it was a relatively brief call. The third time I picked the phone up from the coffee table, I heard a dial tone.

The weather report was next and it always riles me up. You'd think that by now the meteorologists would have their act together. They seem to have a good handle on yesterday's weather and what it's like outside when they are talking, but forecasting is more of a challenge than it should be. It's not like the weather is trying to baffle them. The clouds and high-pressure areas aren't approaching the area like a soccer player trying to outsmart a goalie.

There was no mention of Pentecost Sunday on the news, so I turned on a religious program that was beginning. That's as close to church as I get these days. The host had a shiny robe and a distinguished beard, and he talked about the day and what it meant. I was distracted by the way everything sounded like he was reading from a script.

I turned on a baseball game, read the newspaper, and did some writing. I forget how I spent Pentecost Sunday last year.

Steve Pastis has written for the *Valley Voice*, *The Good Life*, *Greek Accent*, *Farm News*, *Custom Boat & Engine*, *Baseball Cards*, *Circus*, *Rock Fever*, *Occidental Magazine*, *Destination Visalia*, *South Valley Networking*, *Hellenic Calendar*, and *Cool and Strange Music*. His stories have been published in *The Journal of Experimental Fiction*, *Signs of Life*, and *Gargoyle*. Four of his short story collections, *Fables for the Clarinet*, *Ten Good Reasons to Fix that Airplane*, *Elk and Penguin Stories*, and *Honey for the Cold War*, are available on Amazon. His book publishing website is at NameYourOwnDuck.com.

MOMMY, IS THERE REALLY A SANTA CLAUS

BOBBIE FITE

"**M**ommy, can I cook, too?"
Ellen pushed a strand of hair out of her eyes with a floured finger and turned to look at her six-year-old daughter. The child's smile and her big, trusting eyes were impossible to resist. Ellen leaned back against the counter and mustered up a smile of her own.

"What would you like to cook, sweetheart?" she asked, hoping against hope that it would be simple, although a quick glance around the kitchen told her that Suzie would have a hard time making any greater mess.

"A pumpkin pie like yours for Santa Claus," Suzie responded. "He is coming tonight, isn't he?"

"That's right. It's Christmas Eve and Santa will definitely be here." And the whole family, all sixteen of them, will be here tomorrow, she added to herself.

In her head, she ran through the list of things that still needed to be done before she would consider herself and her home ready for company. Except for the kitchen, the house was clean. All of the decorations were up, the dressing was ready, the bird nearly defrosted, and the pie crusts rolled. Her mom and sisters were bringing the rest of dinner. Jim wouldn't be home until five thirty, which gave her a little over an hour to finish the pies, clean the kitchen, take a shower, put on some makeup, fix her hair, get dressed, get Suzie ready, and pick up three-year-old Joey from his play date next door before they needed to leave for church. Thank goodness they'd decided to grab hamburgers on the way to the candlelight service, so at least she didn't have to worry about cooking dinner. All things considered she could handle one more little pie.

She let out a sigh and brought her attention back to her daughter. "Wash your hands, then find one of those little pans in the bottom drawer. I'll have plenty of left-over dough for you in a minute. When it's ready, we'll cook your pie in the oven with the big pies."

Suzie's look of delight as she dove for the junk drawer brought Ellen her first real smile of the busy afternoon. "Hey! Go wash your hands first," she reminded her daughter before getting back to work on the apple pie's lattice top.

Ellen finished pinching the edges of her last pumpkin-pie shell while watching Suzie try to roll out the dough for her four-inch pie. The rolling pin was too much for the little hands, and the dough kept curling up around it and getting stuck. Suzie glanced at Ellen and caught her grinning. The look of concentration fled and the little girl began to giggle. She pushed the rolling pin away, rolled the dough into a ball with her hands, pounded it flat on the table and squished it into the little pan with her fingers.

"There!" Suzie said. "Do you think Santa will like it?"

"Of course," Ellen replied. "He loves pie. How do you think he got so fat?" She chuckled, until it occurred to her that this particular pie would be adding to her own waistline. She'd be sure to split it with Jim, after describing in detail how it came to be.

Ellen mixed a couple of cans of pumpkin with the rest of the ingredients, getting a bit of messy help with the eggs, and filled her pie shells, then she handed the bowl to her daughter. Suzie's face became solemn as she spooned the last of the mix into the little pie shell for Santa Claus, and Ellen found herself frowning in sympathy. It was rare to see her daughter anything but happy and carefree. Her open, cheerful, trusting nature was one of the qualities that made her so endearing.

"Mommy?" Suzie said, without looking up. Her voice was quiet, hesitant. "Is there really a Santa Claus?"

Did she hear tears in Suzie's voice? Ellen's throat constricted and she felt the warmth of tears collecting in her own eyes. It was a delicate question. The first really tough one she'd had to face. It represented the first step into an adult world she wasn't sure either of them was ready for.

There was so much more involved than a simple yes or no. Would Suzie understand the tradition and the joy, or simply think she'd been lied to? Would she understand how much a part of everyone's Christmas, young and old, that jolly old elf really was, or just think the fun had been lost? Would she understand...?

Ellen had known the question would come up eventually, and she had even considered what her answer might be, but maybe this wasn't the best time. She was beat, and there was so much still to do to get ready for the big day tomorrow.

"Of course, there's really a Santa Claus," she answered, knowing she was evading the question. "Why do you ask?"

"Some of the big kids were talking after school. They said that Santa was make-believe, just for babies, and that parents really put out the presents." Suzie's eyes met Ellen's. The little girl was old enough to ask a hard question, and she obviously expected an answer. There was no way to avoid giving it to her. Ellen took a deep breath.

"It is parents who put out the presents," she said, watching carefully for her daughter's reaction. "But that doesn't make Santa make-believe. He may not live at the North Pole, or drive a sleigh with flying reindeer, but he is alive in everyone's hearts. In many forms, he brings gifts of love to children all over the world, just like the wise men brought gifts for the baby Jesus. You remember that story."

Solemnly, Suzie nodded. Ellen sat down and pulled the little girl into her arms. She prayed her words were making sense. She couldn't really tell from the look on Suzie's face.

"You have to remember that the first Christmas was the day when God gave us the greatest gift of all. He gave us His Son to show us the way to a better life. That is really why we celebrate Christmas. So even if you never see a fat little man in a red suit come down the chimney, and even if it is mothers and fathers, or grandparents, aunts, uncles and other people, who deliver the gifts for Santa, Santa is real and he tells us every year that we are loved."

Suzie tilted her head to the side and looked at Ellen for a moment, then slid off her lap and smiled. "That's what I thought," she said. "When's the pie gonna be done?"

Ellen's heart sank and tears threatened again, so she took a deep breath and mentally shrugged. Better luck next time, she told herself. At least the child is still smiling. She couldn't have handled tears or the sulks at the moment. Maybe Jim would have some better ideas for the next time Suzie asked.

"It'll be done in about half an hour, sweetie. Then we have to get ready for church."

"Okay," Suzie said, smiled again and skipped away toward her room humming what sounded like *"Here Comes Santa Claus."*

* * *

"Mommy? Daddy? Are you awake? Santa Claus was here!" Suzie whispered in a voice that was almost a shout. Her little brother stood beside her, his eyes shining with excitement. Ellen snuggled up against her husband's shoulder and pulled the blanket over their heads, sharing a smile with Jim as he peeked out at their children.

"Mommy! Daddy!" Suzie whispered again. "Come on! It's morning."

"Are you sure?" Ellen poked her husband in the ribs to keep him from laughing out loud, then pulled the covers down enough to look at the two excited youngsters. "It's still dark."

"It's six thirty. Come on!" Suzie grabbed Joey's hand and they jumped onto the bed to pull the covers down and drag their not-really-reluctant parents out.

Finally, dressed in robes and slippers, the four of them entered the living room. Jim turned on the lights to the Christmas tree, transforming the room into the magical place the children had waited so impatiently for. Suzie and Joey dashed to the tree where Santa had left their special gifts, wrapped only in bows, with big tags naming the new owners. They squealed and giggled and showed off to each other and to their parents. Finally, remembering their stockings, they headed toward the fireplace.

"Oh, look!" Suzie cried. "Mommy, Daddy, there are two extra stockings here. They must be for you."

Ellen looked across the room to see the two new stockings taped to the mantel as though Santa had left them. She crossed the room and took down all four stockings. There were the two made of red felt and fur that the children had hung before going to bed, now filled with tiny toys, candy and nuts. Then, there were two more, made of red construction paper, sewn together with yarn and decorated with crayon and glitter. On one appeared the carefully printed name "ELEN," on the other was "JIM."

The little stinker, Ellen thought. Pressing her lips together to try to keep the tears at bay, she handed Christmas stockings to her children and husband, then sat down to admire her own. A quick glance around showed Jim next to her, head down, carefully examining his stocking, Joey tearing open a candy wrapper, and Suzie watching both parents with a shy, expectant smile. Inside the stocking, Ellen found a small card with a picture of Santa Claus drawn on the front. The message, also carefully printed, said: "Santa Loves You Too."

Bobbie Fite lives outside of Sacramento, California. She has a story about her summer vacation in Colorado in the NCPA "Destination the World, Vol 2" anthology, and is the author of three novels. In her first book, Lauren's *Nightmares* may be more than just bad dreams. Could she be witnessing actual crimes? In her historical novel, *Sunshine and The Bounty Hunter*, the title character has a bright smile, but no memory of her past. Why she was riding across the dangerous Wyoming prairie alone? Finally, *Storm Damage* takes place two days before Christmas when the roof of a busy shopping mall collapses. Buried in the debris are a young widow, a frustrated cop, a displaced great-grandmother and an abandoned child. They could wait for rescue, but buried with them is a killer with a great deal to lose. For more information, visit Bobbie's website: www.bobbiefite.com.

CHRISTMAS WITH CATS
NORMA JEAN THORNTON

Baked breads and cookies - sweet candies and pies
Aromas and sights fill our noses and eyes

Cinnamon, sage and other spice
They always make a house smell nice

Leftover batter from cakes, the kids taste
It's always too good to let go to waste

Samplin' and pickin' at the ham and turkey
The cats want some too, but they prefer jerky

Wrapping the presents, with help from the cats
You just wish they'd go out and chase some rats

Decorating the tree – the cats help there, too
If they were a dog, they could go chase a shoe

The cats will run up and down the tree
Knock ornaments off and run with glee

They try to chew light cords. and get tangled in string
But you can't get mad, they're just doin' their cat thing

They scratch things, slap at, and tear stuff all down
And all you can do is just watch and frown

You love 'em to pieces, except when they're brats
But they never will mind, those silly old cats

A TRILOGY OF HOLIDAY CELEBRATIONS IN THE PHILIPPINES

CHRISTINE "CHRISSI" L. VILLA

Half an Hour Away from *Noche Buena*

The voices of children carolers jolted me from my deep sleep. Tambourines made of bottle caps shook louder and louder while coins rattled in tin cans. The children were singing, "Thank you, thank you, *ang babait ninyo* (you are so kind), thank you!"

I squinted my eyes and peered through the darkness. The clock ticked loudly. I looked up and found it perched on my side table. As it read 11:30, my heart somersaulted. It was half an hour away from *Noche Buena*, the traditional Filipino Christmas eve family feast!

Slowly poking my head through the door, I peeked and tiptoed to the top of the staircase. The house was unusually quiet. Perhaps, everybody had gone to the Midnight Mass except for Grandma. I could hear her switching pans and stirring pots. The aroma of roasted garlic, peanut butter sauce, and shrimp paste filled the house. As I scurried down the stairs like a mouse on the well-polished wooden steps, I could sniff the smell of *tsokolate* (thick Spanish cocoa) brewing from the kitchen.

I sat in the middle of the stairs, between the carved banisters, and ogled at our long dining table. On the center of the table, fruits of every color of the rainbow were piled high in a rattan basket. Glass dishes overflowed with noodles. Some noodles blended with bite-sized hotdogs and tomato sauce. Other noodles twisted around shredded chicken and chopped vegetables. On the other side of the table, a big slab of glazed ham was eagerly waiting to be carved. In a silver bowl, a fluffy white cream unevenly coated chunks of fruits and tiny marshmallows. I sneaked around the table to dip my finger in it. Licking its sweetness and snatching one bite of crunchy lumpia (egg roll), which lay among the other miniature logs on the banana leaf, was enough to send me to heaven!

In our living room, the Christmas tree, adorned with red Christmas balls and gold velvet bows, towered above me. Its soft, multicolored lights twinkled alternately. Under the tree, glossy, colorful boxes beamed at me. I placed a small box close to my ear and jiggled it twice.

Suddenly, I heard the kitchen door squeak. I raced back to my dark bedroom and watched the string of lights, draped around the eaves of our house, glow like fireflies. I felt the cold air tickling my cheeks. In a short while, a whiff of burnt powder traveled towards my nostrils. I looked down and saw two boys scratching *watusi* (firecrackers) on the ground with their rubber slippers. The watusi sparkled, crackled, danced around, and emitted smoke in the air.

Next thing I knew, there was noisy chatter in the house. As I heard footsteps running up the stairs, I rushed to my bed and covered myself with a blanket. Somebody burst in and turned on the light.

"Wake up! Wake up! It's time for *Noche Buena!*" yelled my brother. He pulled the blanket back and slowly unfolded before me a banana leaf in his hands. Inside were two purple rice cakes, topped with dripping melted butter and sprinkles of coconut mixed with sugar.

before bedtime
Father dusts
Mother's photograph
I write another wish list
for next Christmas

"Half an Hour Before *Noche Buena*" is a *tanka* prose, a literary form that combines prose and tanka. The tanka may be placed in the beginning, middle, or end. It is vital that the prose and tanka stand on their own and when combined, there is an effective juxtaposition between both.

Tanka, meaning 'short song', is the modern name for *waka*, 'Japanese song', the traditional form of unrhymed five-line lyric poetry which originated many years ago in Japan. Still written in five lines with usually a total number of thirty-one or fewer syllables, observing a short, long, short, long, long pattern, contemporary tanka embraces a wide range of human experiences. Like the sonnet, tanka pivots between seemingly two unrelated parts. This unexpected turn marks the link and shift from a concrete image, idea, or event, to a personal response. Tanka verses do not have titles unless they are in a tanka sequence.

The following is a tanka sequence about a holiday celebrated in the Philippines.

Remembering Grandpa

Araw ng Kagitingan*
rows of white crosses
where Grandpa rests . . .
Father begins his soliloquy
only he can hear

family squabbles
about Grandpa's will
his grave
surprisingly, filled with flowers
wilted and new

Father brushes
the faded inscriptions
on the cross . . .
he breaks the silence
with untold war stories

how many Japanese soldiers
did Grandpa kill?
up to now
I mostly treasure the name
he used to call me

no longer able
to pay respects
by kissing his hand
I offer him strings
of *sampaguita***

*Araw ng Kagitingan means National Hero's Day.
**Sampaguita, also known as Philippine Jasmine, is a fragrant flower often made into a garland of welcome for decoration or adornment of religious images or photographs of the dead, etc.

The following poem is a *cherita* sequence about a holiday tradition observed in the Philippines. *Cherita* is a six-line poem that tells a story. The founder of cherita, ai li says, "*Cherita* is the Malay word for story or tale. A cherita consists of a single stanza of a one-line verse, followed by a two-line verse, and then finishing with a three-line verse. It can be written solo or with up to three partners. Like tanka verses, cherita poems do not have titles unless they are in a cherita sequence. The cherita sequence below is composed of *cherita terbalik*. *Cherita terbalik* can be written in these stanza formats—(1-3-2), (2-1-3), (2-3,1), (3-1-2), or (3-2-1).

Memories of *Semana* Santa

on Palm Sunday

Step-Mom takes home
blessed palm branches
as trophy for attending mass

the day I question
what our tradition is all about

*

the malls are closed
radio and tv shows
are off the air

two half-sisters
squabbling in the pool

when does real praying start?

*

from a distance
a chanting of religious verses
until 2 a.m.

teasing and taunting me
the summer heat becomes
more unbearable

*

*Banal na Huwebes*** and *Biyernes Santo****
a non-working holiday
to visit 7 churches

my brother and I giggle
as Step-Mom leads the Station of the Cross

how much do we need to repent?

*

caught eating meat
I am judged to be a sinner

only fish is allowed
during Holy Week,
they say
we eat quietly over every meal

*

finally, it's Palm Sunday

groceries are open
karaoke music in full blast

once again
Father and Step-Mom
start their bickering

*Semana Santa means Holy Week.
**Banal na Huwebes means Holy Thursday.
***Biyernes Santo means Good Friday.

Christine "Chrissi" L. Villa founded *Purple Cotton Candy Arts*, a small business that started exploring in the field of arts and crafts, later expanding into publishing her children's picture books.

She has published eleven children's books since 2014, winning first place in both 2018 and 2019 NCPA Book Award Competitions, plus silver in 2020, for Children's Books and Cover Design & Inner Layout categories, with *Will You Still Love Me? A Puppy Haiku Story.*

Purple Cotton Candy Arts now offers publishing services to aspiring children's authors and publishers.

As a gifted poet, Chrissi's haiku and tanka have appeared in numerous online and print journals worldwide, garnering several awards.

Chrissi:
published her first poetry book *The Bluebird's Cry.*
is founding editor of Frameless Sky, the first haiku and tanka journal available on DVD, and Velvet Dusk Publishing.
is new editor of Ribbons, the official publication of Tanka Society of America
www.christinevilla.com.

THE POOR MAN AND THE ACTRESS
LINDA VILLATORE

Based on a true story from the north woods.

One time, not long before Christmas, a young woman who was very sad decided that she would join a troupe of actors and take on the role of someone else. In this way she thought she might become happy again.

She went to a nearby town where there was a well-known troupe of actors and a marvelous theatre. It was exciting to see. She went in, put down her name, and joined many others waiting to be tested. In her turn, she stood in front of the director of the troupe and read from a small red book. Inside the book a story was being told through only the speaking voice of each character. She was nervous, but read aloud the voice of characters, as she was asked.

Though she had little experience, the director saw that she could pretend this way and read with conviction. He selected her and gave her two small roles: a child in a pink dress, excited to see her gifts, and a vain young woman in a posh blue gown at a party.

The play itself was a well-known Christmas story of a selfish man who sees his future through the eyes of three ghosts and decides to become a better and more generous man. He too was sad and lonely, so the young woman understood the situation. She had pity on him. Perhaps she had pity for herself as well.

The weather grew colder. It rained every day and the theatre was damp. Yet the troupe of actors worked happily to prepare their play. They met in the empty theater and pretended to be the townspeople in the story. They got more convincing each week.

While the actors learned to memorize speech and move about on the stage, another group cut, sawed, painted and hammered away making scenery. It was marvelous!

Fifty people worked together.

All the scenery was designed to unfold from three Christmas ornaments suspended from the ceiling. These ornaments were as big as houses; one in gold, one red and one green, and like all ornaments, they sparkled with gold braid. But unlike other ornaments these opened and closed, and could be slowly turned. Throughout the play the scenes would unfold from them. While the play came to life, the actors could move across the stage as the ornaments transformed themselves.

Day by day the story became more real to the actors and to the sad young woman. One day she realized she was not sad anymore. It seems she had moved something else into her mind. And there was a feeling of community among members of the troupe. Together, they grew excited about the progress of their work. They began to look forward with pride to sharing it with people who would come to see their play, created from nothing but a small red book.

Then, just before Christmas on a cold and dreary day, the opening day of the play arrived. People were invited. There would be an audience. She was filled with excitement.

But as it can sometimes do, life took a new turn. On her way to the theatre that special day, she happened to pass a young man sitting at the side of the road. He was dressed in baggy brown clothes. His head was down. He was too near the traffic. He looked forlorn. She understood how he could be sad having nothing and living in such cold. She decided to stop and speak with him in the time she had.

As she stopped, she suddenly had an idea. She would invite him to see the play!

She approached him softly and explained...she was on her way to take part in a play. It was in the next town. She invited him to come along as her guest of honor. To her surprise the man agreed. He got in the warm car and sat quietly...thinking about what...she did not know.

His name was Peter.

They arrived at the still empty theatre. She introduced Peter to the director and told him of her plan. To her delight, the director approved. With that, she took Peter up onto the stage and showed him the imaginary village they had created. She showed him the three ornaments in gold, red and green and explained how they worked. Then with a few minutes to spare, she brought Peter a cup of hot coffee and pastry. She made sure he was comfortable in the back of the theatre. He was shy. He sat quietly sipping his hot coffee and waited for the play to begin.

She left to put on her make-up and first costume: a pink dress, bonnet and shiny black shoes.

The lights came up, and as the play began, she forgot about Peter. Dutifully, she played her part in the spectacle. With the others, she was carried by the dream of story they had created from nothing. It all unfolded as planned, even the ornaments, and a greedy man was made whole and spread his kindness through the town on Christmas morning.

As the curtain came down and the applause subsided, she looked out for Peter and found him still in his seat. But now he was applauding from his place in the back of the theater. He had stayed. He had forgotten his sorrows enough to enjoy this particular day. The play had worked its magic. So, with light, music and color, he had taken part in many other lives. For a brief time, he was in another time. The story in the red book, so different than the one he was living, had entered his heart. It carried his imagination as it had done for the young woman. She saw him smiling.

She changed back into her own clothes and went out to find him. Peter was gone. He had left without saying good bye. He must have walked through the departing crowd alone. But in his shyness, he was holding the gift. Hope.

It does no harm to imagine that a greedy man can become a loving one, or that peace can be found among people at work on a project they love. His chest could have felt warmer from these thoughts.

Hope is warm. It glows in the chest. Once lit, it requires no thanks. Hope sits quietly in a stricken heart where it works its magic. Each one of us needs an escape from the rigors of the world, to restore our hearts, even if only for a short while. And for a short while, that is enough.

Linda Villatore is an award-winning educator with over 30 years of experience in custom web based and classroom instructional design and training. She is author of several acclaimed activity-based courses and published in multi-media, staffing and production magazines. She is an award-winning dramatic actress and stage director, as well as a documentary television producer with high-level expertise in communication and media production. Linda now specializes in executive coaching, strategic planning, facilitation, and project management.

She has taught in universities, community colleges, the public and private sector for clients in over 40 industries. She was awarded by the U. S. Army for educational counseling, and nominated for the California *Governor's Award for Environmental Economic Leadership, Who's Who* in *American Colleges and Universities.*

Linda played competition chess with Bobbie Fischer at the age of seven.

Master of Fine Arts in Directing
BA Liberal Studies
Multimedia Project Management Certification Bay Area Video Coalition (BAVC)
http://lindavillatore.com/

LEAVES OF FALL—
A HOLIDAY MESSAGE
BARBARA KLIDE

Well-lived people wise in their way
Be present they say, in the zone every day
Be grateful, be kind, do what makes your heart sing.

The fall leaves of nature have their messaging too
A blaze of golds, reds, oranges our eyes excited by hues
Enjoy today they shout, from all directions, to you.

But turning brown, dropping fast they will not last
An awakening, a reminder, do not procrastinate
Urging us, indeed don't wait, don't hesitate.

Absorb their striking beauty now
To nurture your soul and remind us how
Be still, be present you must allow.

∞

Thanksgiving came with leaves of fall
The memory remains like contrails for all
On plates the next day and into nightfall.

Soon, we will plan to mark more days
Christmas and Hanukkah are a few of the ways
Enjoying, grateful to "be" in the now I vow.

Gratefulness our warrior, to ward off each beast
Of our stray and wearisome thoughts and concerns
A sheepdog keeping our minds at peace.

∞

2020 rose a mammoth storm, yet we found our grace
Ring in the New Year—approaching with haste,
Buds and blooms of spring following, taking its place

The fall leaves still here, walk by them don't wait
Absorb their power, their vital message, this hour
To move and balance, give thanks, celebrate.

HIBERNATING CHRISTMAS

A.K. BUCKROTH

t's time, people. It is time to put Christmas away. "Away" is the key word. Face it. I hate to admit – or go through the rigorous endeavors of having to do it – but "it" must be done. Putting it – the collection of years and years of decorations – on display, is always happy fun, great memories galore, all good things. BUT…they all *have* to be put away.

As I scan the dense collection of Christmas paraphernalia populating our living room, the stereo must go on, lightly beating with my favorite rock music. *Thump, thump, thump.* As my husband is able to escape to a job, this goal is mine to behold. I am in charge (laughter permissible). With a cup of warm hibiscus tea in hand, I envision another grand plan.

This three-bedroom, two bath house on 1/3 of an acre of land has had Christmas all over itself year in and year out, inside *and* out. It plainly blows up!

Unexcited at my movements throughout the house, our dog surprisingly lays quiet on his pillow bed, steadily watching me, his large, dark eyes move from side to side as I move. Unusual for a Parsons Terrier, I believe he must be used to seeing me do this year after year, at least the last ten years of his life. He doesn't move his head, only his eyes. Not only that, but he knows better than to interrupt or disturb my focus, my concentration. He is smart to stay in one place.

To begin, our 20+ year old home-made patch-work Christmas quilt is delicately removed from the back of the couch. After slumbering there for a month, it is delicately laundered, folded, then packed away in an air tight, zippered plastic bag. No moths allowed. Next, the decorative Christmas pillows gently go through the same process, stored in the same bag. Done. My happy adrenaline rushes with that simple accomplishment, ready to conquer this next re-packing Christmas feat.

Adventuring further into the living room, the lonely looking, scenically embroidered large, empty Christmas stockings continue to hang on the mantel with so much loving care. Gosh, each holds memories of chocolates, perfumes, jewelry, toothbrushes, shaving essentials and numerous other toiletries that "Santa Claus" has stuffed into each one, gifting us humble residents. Grateful for such supplies, we feel secure with these daily items. The stockings are easily removed from their colorful and purposeful mantel-born hooks and become an addition to the large, two-foot by three-foot blue, hard plastic box with its matching cover. The Christmas tree skirt displaying a delicate scene of a snow-covered forest lays folded on the floor awaiting its safe bundling. Organizing this chaos has begun. Numerous color-coded, stackable boxes help keep my brain organized as well for next year. There's always next year. Together, they await a neat packing before being stored one upon the other in the outside shed.

There is a method to my madness. I'm not really insane; it just seems like it. "OCD," Obsessive Compulsive Disorder, is more the mild ailment for my habitual and neat organizing skills.

Next, the decorative Christmas kitchen and bath hand towels will become an addition to that same container after being used to wipe down kitchen counters, the refrigerator, dining room table and such. Heck, they make good cleaning cloths! The special Christmas patterned hot pan holders, cloth napkins and table cloths, are inclusive in one laundry cycle before being packed. Add a few moth balls, and I'm happy as the chaos continues to become a win-win situation.

Then there are the Christmas trees. There are two of these – one inside, one out. Such decorative tasks hold more love upon their beginnings. At the holiday's finale, it takes more than a few days to take them apart separately. The outside one, mostly due to, and dependent upon, the weather. Wind, rain and lower temperatures are not only uncomfortable to disassemble a decorated pine tree, but frustrating when I want and need to get this done. And having to climb that eight-foot ladder to undecorate this specific tree again, in the mud, just is not going to happen. Time is also of the essence. I'd like to have this all neatly put away before New Year's Eve! However, this goal is not always attained.

The outside tree decorations can always wait a few more days. They have to. After all, I did a beautiful job decorating it if I say so myself. My neighbors remain in awe. I rather like it myself, so it can keep its oversized bobbles and sparkles a little longer. Truly, I do not look forward to dragging out the eight-to-ten-foot aluminum ladder to accomplish this task. This handsome and poignant blue spruce in the front yard, planted in April of 2005, is now a beautiful and healthy ten-foot-tall, on the property's edge. This task involves removing multiple red ribbons, bows, six-inch and eight-inch round, and shimmering, plastic globes, along with at least six yards of white and gold beaded garlands. I did not forget to place shimmering silver tinsel on every limb of this beauty. I've decided that the tinsel can remain to flutter in the wind. It sparkles nicely. Lastly, four strings of multi-colored lights get unplugged first, before tackling the temporary yet dizzying effect of being unwound, zip-tied into neatness, and boxed.

The four window wreaths can wait a little longer along with the colorful display of blinking roof lights which surely can be seen from space. However, the continual twinkling of red, blue, yellow, green, white and purple LED lights will come to a well-deserved and prolonged rest. The neighbors will be thankful, I'm sure.

The inside tree becomes undressed a little at a time in passing. A novel bulb here, a Noel bell there, etc., will be removed – sooner or later. Their Christmas storage boxes separately stand in the hall awaiting all members. The 'precious' artifacts from decades past will remain until the very last. Loving care is tender in time. These decorations require four separate plastic tubs which will also be stacked one upon the other in the backyard shed.

For example, the hand blown and painted glass balls from Poland are given special attention due to their delicate, egg-shell nature. Or the ever-so-delicate penguin ornament, a gift from a precious friend, becomes ensconced in protective layers of tissue paper. The even more-delicate Hawaiian shirt ornaments, remembrances of a trip to Hawaii, so thin in composition, also require a delicate touch when handling. In addition, the crystal chimes in memory of our visit to the Westwood Crystal Manufacturing Plant in Ireland, are carefully bubble-wrapped and packed. Ah, such glory! Not only do these items require more attentive packing and sealing, but they are the most joyous – personal.

Included in this particularly protective box are the most favorite and special ornaments – you know, the ones your kids made in grade school. One is a geometrical-shaped whatchamacallit of different-colored construction papers with a personal photo of our daughter at age five or six glued on one angle. Another is a popsicle stick-thingy colored with magic markers. My favorite is the five-inch red flannel teddy bear figure with glued-on eyeballs and a small blue flannel scarf. A small magnet pasted on its back allows it to stay on the refrigerator for everyone to enjoy. Precious. Our daughter put a lot of love into this character. These items will hibernate with the ones from Europe. They are all about the same age. Mm hmm, good memories.

The tree skirt gets delicately folded and added to the Christmas linen box, so labeled. It is not laundered. I have a fear of its snow sparkles getting washed down the drain. Not a good thought.

The porcelain, multi-character nativity and its scenery needs extra loving care. Each piece of fifteen symbolic and historical figurines are ever-so-carefully wrapped in fabric swaths, secured with packing tape, placed in their separate and original Styrofoam containers, then laid in a grey plastic tub.

Once the packing boxes are tightly closed with refreshed labels, they are placed one atop the other, awaiting outdoor shed placement. Then the finish – the fake tree is taken apart, limb by limb, all securely tucked into its original box and placed on top of the tubs. Bittersweet, really. Like a Christmas in reverse.

Of all this Christmas stuff, my favorite has been dressing the outside tree.

Ah, I'm tired now. Just thinking and planning all this as I share it with you means another positive end-of-year goal has been accomplished! Now, my part is done. Hubby's part will be to carry each of these eight tubs into the shed. Did I count that right? What's next for me? Readying for the next celebration...my birthday!

Happy New Year!

 A.K. Buckroth is a member of the Northern California Publishers and Authors (NCPA), where she has continued to be encouraged, motivated and emotionally supported in her writing endeavors.

As a T1D (Type One/Juvenile Diabetic), her books reflect a prosperous life with this disease. Her first, *My Diabetic Soul – An Autobiography* ©2010 (Revised 2018), brought her numerous awards from Boston, MA, Worcester, MA, Indianapolis, IN, and Sacramento, CA. Personally recorded, it is available via Audio.com, along with paperback and e-book versions.

She has also written: *Me and My Dog Named Money...a child's story of diabetes* Revised ©2019, *Me & My Money Too Book Two* Revised ©2019, and *Kisses for Cash...T1D meets T2D Book Three* ©2016 which received an NCPA award.

In addition, Andrea has a story in three other NCPA anthologies: *Birds of a Feather* ©2019, and *DESTINATION: The World Vol 1 & 2,* both ©2020.

www.mydiabeticsoul.com and #buckroth.

HOW OUR FAMILY CELEBRATED THE CHRISTMAS HOLIDAY

EMMA CLASBERRY

When growing up as a child, Christmas was the greatest holiday our family and other families in the community celebrated. It was a day of thanksgiving to God for keeping them alive throughout the year, and for the birth of His son, Jesus Christ. It was when sons, unmarried daughters, wives, husbands and other relatives came home from far and near to celebrate together with their families.

We, Nigerian-Ibibio people, call this day, '*Ekom Obong*, which means, '[All] Thank the Lord (God)'. It was usually a day of joy. And any family who had a child born into the family on that day had the option to name the child, Ekom Obong. My mother gave birth to a daughter on one Christmas Day, and my father named her, Ekom Obong. This traditional practice may still continue till today.

Families prepared for Christmas Day celebration individually and collectively. They prepared for it mentally, financially and socially as well. And the community as a whole was not left out in this preparation.

How my father prepared for Christmas Day

Being blessed financially and as a minister of God, my father did not want to spoil his children by lavishing on us, buying expensive clothing for us. He did not want us to be arrogant or feel different just because our parents were affluent. He wanted us to blend with other children and focus on our education. That orientation was cool then and has really helped me in many ways up till today.

But for Christmas gifts, my father bought expensive and

beautiful new outfits for his children. About a month before Christmas day, he would buy yards of fabric of different designs for new dresses to be made for us to wear to church on Christmas day. Sometimes, he bought us ready-made dresses, if he was late in buying fabric and the time for the tailor to sew the dresses was short. For us girls, he bought hats and sometimes shoes also.

For us children, Christmas was the day to display our new dresses, shoes and hats. There was no Christmas my father missed giving us new clothing, new hats, and sometimes, shoes too. I was always looking forward to this Great Day. I enjoyed these treats by my father up to when I left home at about eighteen years old to attend Police Training College in Lagos, Nigeria.

Children, whose parents could not afford them new dresses would be sad, and some would cry and refuse to be comforted. So, parents did their best to give their children at least new dresses, even if they could not afford to buy them shoes and hats in addition.

My father usually bought nice outfit for himself for Christmas too. But I don't remember seeing him buy any outfit for my mother as Christmas gift, as many other husbands did for their wives. But whenever my mother had a baby, he usually decked her with the most expensive fashion in vogue in town to thank her for bearing a child for him, and to wear to church for the Christening/blessing of the baby by a church minister.

My father was also responsible for buying big food items for Christmas dinner. He would buy items like long dried stock fish (cod fish), a rack of five pairs of large dried fish, chicken and goat meats, and big yams. The quantity of yams he bought depended on how many extended family members would attend the Christmas get-together.

Which extended family members usually attended?

My father usually hosted the Christmas Day celebration. So, all roads led to our house. My parents had eight children. My father's brother had a wife and seven

143

children. His two half-brothers had two wives each, and five children. The number of attendees typically fluctuated. It could be more one Christmas, and less at another.

How my mother prepared for Christmas Day

My mother usually prepared for the day in particular. While my father bought the big items, my mother took care of all other ingredients for the soup and the dinner in general.

My mother also made sure there would be enough food for the family throughout that Christmas week. From Christmas Day to New Year's Day, the whole week was regarded as a holiday period, when community members rested from farm work, celebrated the birth of Christ, reserved energy and prepared for the up-coming farming season.

My mother did not buy any clothing for my dad for that purpose either. The general practice or expectation was that it was the responsibility of the husbands to give their wives some new dresses as Christmas gifts. She did not quite understand why my father chose not to buy her any dress for Christmas, as other husbands in the community did for their wives.

She was not fussy about it nor ever confronted my father for not giving her Christmas dress, as other wives did to their husbands. But since my father took up the sole responsibility to give his children Christmas dresses, my mother was satisfied with that, given the fact that some fathers did not meet that responsibility for their children at Christmas.

For Christmas, my mother usually bought some clothing for herself. Any Christmas she could not afford it, she wore her old dress to church that day. [Note that then, the items for Christmas gifts were mainly food, cooked or raw, and clothing.]

The whole community prepared for the day

Young men in the community made sure the big village park was cleared and made ready for the Christmas dance festival.

Drummers prepared their drums, shined them and made sure they were in good condition. Many bought new T-shirts and wrappers specifically to wear on that day. Other instrumentalists prepared in like manner. Young men who would lead in singing also prepared their songs. Even community members who planned to dance made sure their T-shirts for the dance were new or in good condition.

For some families, that was when to repair their houses. They painted the walls if the original paint was beginning to fade off, or plastered the walls and the floors with fresh mud, if they lived in mud houses. Women/wives usually did the plastering, while husbands/men repaired house roofs if need be.

Activities on Christmas Day

In the morning, as early as 5am, women and children (7 years old and up) went to the stream to fetch water. Sometimes, the children went to the stream twice that morning to fetch water so there would be enough water for all the cooking that would be done that day, while my mother would stay back to prepare breakfast.

Before breakfast was ready, my father would send me out with baskets of food items, such as five big yams, stockfish, five pairs of big smoked fish and other food items, as Christmas gifts to take to two or three of his family friends.

The recipients were particularly those whom my parents knew were really poor, including a couple of widows, and could not afford Christmas delicacies. I usually carried the baskets on my head, one basket for one person at a time, walking on foot about one quarter to half a mile, to take the gifts to those people. The number of trips depended on the number of recipients.

Breakfast was now ready. My father was served first in his dining room as usual. Then we, including my mother, had ours in the kitchen.

Right after, we dressed up in our new outfits. We left for church. I and my mother carried on our heads two basins full of farm proceeds for harvest givings in the church.

Our hats were made of soft fabric, and sometimes made of straw. The soft fabric ones allowed me to carry the load on my head. But if I had straw one, I carried the hat in my hand until I got to the church, and put it on after I put down the load.

I usually sang in the church choir

There was one song that was always sung on Christmas Day. We called the song 'Echo Song'. But the first line of the song is, "While shepherds watched their flocks by night."

I still remember what happened one Christmas. Right after this song was sung, my father could not hold in how that song made him feel inside. He was so inspired by the song that he said in a loud voice, sitting in front of the congregation as usual, "This song touches my spirit and my soul. I wish I could die right now."

He was so moved spiritually by the song that he added that if he died at that moment, he would go straight to heaven. Everyone in the church felt the same way and loved the Echo song. Christmas songs by the choir were not complete without this Echo song.

Preparation of Christmas dinner on that day

After returning from church, my mother, with the help of one or two extended family members, including young males who would pound the yam into fufu/dough, began to prepare the traditional Christmas dish called, *Usung Udia ye Afia Efere'*, which literally means, 'Pounded yam (fufu or yam dough) and white soup'.

Here, pounded yam is like mashed potatoes. It is thicker or firmer. But it is not as soft as mashed potatoes. It is more like bread dough. It is eaten by cutting a small piece, dipping it in the soup and swallowing it.

'White soup' means soup with no red palm oil (nor vegetables) in it as ingredients. The soup is like gravy. It could be thick or light. It is usually thickened by dissolving cooked pounded yam in the soup.

This dish is not an everyday meal for many families, especially for the less-privileged. It is one of the top-notch delicacies, if prepared accordingly, in my culture, Nigerian-Ibibio.

The major ingredients in the soup for this special Christmas dinner are stock fish and big *'inaha'* fish, both of which are rarely part of everyday meals for many families. Chicken or/and goat meats could be added to the soup. When goat meat is added to the soup, the soup is called *'Afia efere ebot*, which means, 'White soup with goat meat in it'.

The meal was now ready to be served. Green plantain leaves were laid out on the floor outside the house at the backyard near to the kitchen to form a platform on which the yam fufu would be placed. By the platform, a low-lying chair was put out for my father to sit on.

It was now time for my father to come into the scene so as to begin serving the people.

In many occasions, I was usually the one sent to go and tell my father that the food was ready. While I went to call my father, others would take their seats. People sat around the food, but not really in a circle.

As soon as my father sat down, able-bodied young men present would roll out from the mortar big balls of pounded yam, still warm, on to the green plantain leaves platform. Each of the balls was about the size of a football. A kitchen knife would be placed by the balls of the pounded yam.

The meats, chicken or/and goat as well as stockfish, other kind of fish, already sorted out and put in separate plates, were placed on the green plantain leaves platform. Serving spoons were put in each plate.

My father now began to share the food. He sliced the yam fufu into triangles as one would slice cheesecake or pie in a round pan, and gave each attendee a slice each. Children's slices were smaller than adults.

Adults had the option to put their yam fufu slices in a plate or carry them in their palms, just as children generally carried theirs in their palms. Some adults chose to leave theirs at one end of the plantain leaves platform, sitting closer to them, and ate from there.

But my father was usually given a plate for his slice and a bowl for the soup. He did not share a plate with anyone, just as some husbands did.

Meanwhile, the pot of soup was still sitting on the fire with low flame so as to remain warm. My mother now delegated younger female to dish out the soup. Two or three people could share a plate of soup. Where possible, mothers shared the soup with their children.

The meats were served last. And my father did the sharing of the meat and fish.

Slices of yam fufu were always surplus. And anyone was free to go for a second round and/or take some left-over food home.

For some extended family members, Christmas Day was a day to eat the most expensive delicacies, a day in a year they knew they would eat until they dropped. Some children ate until they could not breathe nor get up. Some slept off with half slice of pounded yam still in their hands.

And Christmas Day was almost the only occasion when my father ate together with his family. And the same trend applied regarding eating together with his extended family members, with very few exceptions.

A family elder retold a story, "A girl who refused to be beautiful"

After eating, my father would leave the scene and the rest of us would continue eating and entertaining ourselves with some weird rumors in the community. In our family in particular, Christmas Day was also a day when some extended family elders loved to retell and attendees expected to hear funny old-time folktales.

I still remember a story retold by a male elder. It was about a girl who did not like her looks. She was not ugly. But she was not satisfied with her physical appearance. She always wished to be the most beautiful girl in the world.

So, she began to pray to be the most beautiful in looks than anyone else in the city. Luckily, she woke up one morning looking different. When she looked at herself in the mirror, she loved what she saw. Sure! She got what she prayed for, beauty.

As the girl grew up into adulthood, she became more beautiful than ever, until she became exceptionally beautiful. And she liked that.

But soon after she became the most beautiful young woman who ever lived, she began to notice how young men were relating to her. Any young man who saw her wanted to have sex with her. She had several near-rape encounters and a few rape incidents.

Because of these undesirable experiences, the girl regretted becoming so beautiful. She was not as happy as she once was when she was not so beautiful. At some point, she could not handle it, the beauty, anymore

So, she began to look for someone to hand her beauty over to. Unfortunately, she did not find anyone who was willing to accept her gift, her beauty. Why?

Everyone in that city knew what it meant to be extremely beautiful. No man wanted to have such a young woman as a wife because of the fear that other men could molest her sexually, even after she had become someone's wife.

She heard stories where some men planned, though unsuccessfully, to eliminate the husbands of such beautiful girls so that the girls would be free for them to mess with sexually at will.

The girl prayed again and hard to return to her former looks. But that never happened. So, she was stuck with her beauty. Worst of all, she could not get a man who was willing to bear the brunt of marrying an exceptionally beautiful woman. Consequently, she remained lonely, childless and unhappy for the rest of her life.

"What do we learn from this story?" the story-teller asked us. "If you dig too deep (into the ground), you will run into a scorpion," he invoked an African proverb.

He ended the story with this advice: We should be satisfied with our looks, and be careful of what we pray or ask for. Moral lessons from this story were particularly drawn to the attention of teenage girls who were present at the family gathering.

Community members entertained themselves

After relaxing for some hours into the evening, community members headed to the community park. Christmas Day was a day when the whole community had the option to meet at the big village park to enjoy themselves, singing and dancing together.

The drummers and other instrumentalists, who already prepared their drums and their new outfits weeks or months before the Great day, were usually the first to be there at the park so as to set up their instruments. Lead-singers were also part of the first set.

Attendance at the traditional dance part of celebration was optional. And dancing was optional as well. Many had no occasion in a whole year to dance nor to have fun in a group. So, Christmas community dance festival was one opportunity they did not want to miss.

While some attended to dance, some came to watch others dance. Some just wanted to attend so as to be part of the fun that swept through the air on that day. Some, mostly women, came to see those with the latest fashion in town.

Others came to hear what had been cooking in terms of gossips and other funny or silly activities going on or that happened that year in the community. Christmas Day was a day to reveal the latest gossips of the year in the form of songs.

The songs echoed those who 'zoomed' whom, who stole what, who committed adultery with who's wife, and who did what to whom that year in the community. The specific names of the culprits were rarely mentioned in the songs. But many community members usually knew those involved.

Being an Elder/Deacon in the church, my father did not usually attend the dance festival, even to go and watch, let alone dance, probably for religious reasons. When European missionaries came, they condemned such traditional dances, and labeled them 'satanic'. But my mother told me that he used to attend the Christmas day dance and danced too, until he became an Elder in the church.

Did my mother attend the dance? Sometimes, she did. But I never saw her dance, probably because she was a deaconess in the church, and for the fact that she was married to a church Elder/Deacon.

So, whenever she attended the dance festival, she went there just to while away time, to see and admire married women whose husbands decked them with the latest fashion in town and to enjoy the funny rumors and gossips reflected in some of the dance songs.

What happened to attendees on day after Christmas

On the day after Christmas, many (mostly children) who attended the Christmas Day celebration had running stomach, either because they ate too much food day before or because they ate some food their stomach was not familiar with.

If the diarrhea continued beyond two days, the affected persons usually took warm plain water enema on the third day. And that would arrest the diarrhea. Such reaction by our stomachs was always expected, and accepted as part of the Christmas fun. It later became the norm. And that was okay.

How my parents celebrated Christmas has affected how I celebrate it today

My parents spoiled me in this regard. I got used to my family inviting others to our house for dinner on Christmas Day. Today, I do not feel comfortable going to anyone's, including my daughter's, house on Christmas Day when invited. I usually feel out of place when I hang around in someone's house on Christmas Day for food.

Nowadays, I tend to enjoy spending Christmas Day by myself and rarely host it. Maybe, for the sake of getting together with family, it is worth attending such celebration.

My father usually hosted Christmas Day get-together. After he passed, no other extended family male elder continued the practice. As a female, my mother, by tradition, could not continue this family practice, even if she could afford financially to host it. It was usually undertaken by a male family elder, who could afford such expensive dinner, and who also loved doing it.

My father hosted Christmas Day dinner not only because he was blessed financially, and was the most senior of his father's four sons. He did it because he loved and enjoyed giving to the needy, particularly, the widows and other less-privileged, and to make them happy.

I am describing how my parents usually celebrated Christmas when I was a child and up to when my father passed. Also, I left to America many years ago. I am not sure whether any aspect of this tradition has been Westernized, modernized or whatever in recent times.

Emma Umana Clasberry has authored many books on African culture. Her works reflect some of the ideas birthed at a Chicago non-profit agency, African Peoples Institute she founded (1990s through 2000s), to promote cultural awareness and pride among youth and to aid them understand how knowledge of their ethnic culture or lack of it can impact their cultural identity, self-esteem and confidence, their education and career choices, and economic welfare and cultural pride of a people.

Emma has been a Subject of Biographical Record in Who's Who of American Women, 21st Edition, 1999/2000, for Significant Contribution to the Betterment of Contemporary Society.

She earned a B.A in Political Science and an M.A. in Urban Planning & Policy from University of Illinois at Chicago, and a Doctor of Education degree from California Coast University.

Other books by Emma: *Culture of Names in Africa...;* *African Culture Through Proverbs*; and more. Amazon; Xlibris.

A PIRATE'S CHRISTMAS

RONALD JAVOR

The ship almost foundered; the seas were so rough,
The crew was still nimble; they had to be tough.
They'd worked hard, although hungry, and sore as could be,
Many days they'd seen naught but white caps and the sea

The life of a pirate is always a fight
And they'd not seen gold ships for many a night.
'Twas end of the year, and the weather was bad
All work with no rest had made all of them mad

The captain enjoined them, "Work harder today
"Tomorrow is Christmas, and then ye shall play!
"We'll eat and drink 'til our bodies are sore,
"And nary a man will want any more."

The morning broke clear, no winds and calm seas
St. Nicholas, it seemed, their labors did please
Breakfast was gruel; the same, hotter, for lunch,
A slice of stale bread just added some crunch

A big diamond carpet; Christmas stars shining bright,
For the holiday meal they had planned for that night.
They'd been gone for so long, their food stores were short
The cook had no more till they landed in port.

But ribbons were hung on the mast like a tree,
And candles were lit at the tables to see.
"A toast," said the captain, "To our last lonely can,
"Here's to peas on our surf, and good swill to each man."

STAR-SPANGLED CARNIVAL '91

BARBARA YOUNG

E very island in the Caribbean celebrates Carnival at a different time, creating a year-round calendar of festivals. Saint John's month of festivities: food, music, parades, pageants and indulgence, culminate annually on the fourth day in July.

Angie was immersed in a jubilant crowd of dancing people. It was *J'ouvert*, the kick-off event for the final day of Carnival. This very early morning street party inched along the narrow street winding through Cruz Bay until, as its Antillean French Créole name implies, daybreak.

The candy-colored, cottage-buildings of the small Caribbean island business district, appeared ghostly gray in the darkness of pre-dawn. But the party splashed glow-stick light and color, and pulsed a rousing rhythm and sound into the otherwise peaceful night.

Beneath the star-spangled sky, she observed, *everyone sparkles!*

Moisture from the warm tropical air clung and glistened on their skin. Droplets jiggled loose from her ringlets of wet hair. Angie giggled and shouted, "Feelin' *irie!*"—a Jamaican slang for good.

As the noisy *melee*—mixture of unrestrained activity—passed the fire station, one fire-mate streamed water from a flashy silver extinguisher into the steamy party to cool the participants.

"Nur-see." Distinct voices occasionally called to Angie above the organic mix of sounds. She didn't know them, but as the newest nurse on-island, which carries a near-celebrity status, they knew her.

Waving, she called back, "*Okay!*"—a local greeting.

Her toasted-marshmallow complexion contrasted the various tones of molasses and chocolate-syrup skin that

surrounded her, making a savory blend—a Carnival delight.
"All o' we are one," the crowd chanted.

Angie continued with the other sweaty bodies
rhythmically bumping and grinding around the seaside town
until numbness from the hours of merriment and penetrating
reggae rhythms overcame her.

Morning reached this western side of the island. The
brightened sky reoriented Angie.

*If I don't get to sleep, I'll surely become a jumbie—
a spirit from Caribbean lore. I have to go-to-come-
back—a riddle-like* local phrase, meaning to leave and
return.

Once home, barely out of her damp clothes, she fell
limp into the deep featherbed mattress, shrouded by a
sheer, white mosquito net.

She'd dreamt of living in the Caribbean since before
nursing school. After working a few years in critical care at
a hometown hospital, then moving to different states as a
contracted, traveling-nurse, she visited Europe, Canada,
Mexico, Hawaii and the Caribbean where she found her
soul-home.

Her eyelids fluttered as she drifted into sleep with a
pleasant feeling of belonging in this community.

After a heavy four-hour nap that passed like moments,
Angie's eyes flung open, thinking she'd overslept. Her feet
throbbed from treading barefoot in the streets, and the buzz
of energy from the *J'ouvert* party still tingled her body.

I'm tired, like I worked all night in ER. Her eyes
sparkled, cheeks bunched-up into a smile, and she
softy spoke, "Except better!"

She sprang into action to meet her nurse-colleague,
Ms. Rowena, at the park in town.

When she got back to Cruz Bay, the parade line-up was
indistinguishable from the commotion of bum-to-bum people
covering the streets, parking areas, and every corner of
town. "What a pistarkle!" Angie said. The frenetic scene
was a perfect example of the Danish Créole expression.

The town held a cacophony of rumbling motors, ferry
boat horn blasts, and church bells, in a curious blend with

high spirits, brightly colored decorations, and bodies jiggling to the soca music—"feeling hot, hot, hot"—which played loudly in the 86-degree, sunny heat.

I must find Ms. Rowena, then something to eat.

"Okay, Miss An-gie!" Ms. Rowena called as Angie passed by.

"Happy Carnival, Ms. Rowena. You're all *sharped-up* with a frangipani in your hair. I thought the parade was supposed to start at noon?"

"Cheez 'n bred, mehson! "

Angie understood the verbal eye-roll paired with the endearing, non-gender pet-name meaning *my child.* It was a friendly maternal poke by Ms. Rowena.

"...This isn't d' States. Down here, you remember? We're on island-time." Ms. Rowena gently groomed Angie to the culture.

"*Okay,*" Angie said. "What are they drinking from the coconut shell?"

"Wah, you never had d' green coconut? Coconut water is good for d' hot Carnival, y' know...and the jelly on the bottom...it's a good t'ing."

Curious and thirsty, Angie joined the line leading to a pickup truck on the roadside.

A West Indian man stood in the truck bed, with a heap of green coconuts. He whacked the top off with one skillful swing of his machete.

"Good afternoon. Thank you for the show, and this treat!" Angie spoke with the man.

His wiry arm outstretched to give her the all-natural, smooth green drinking vessel with a straw and little purple umbrella.

"Mmm, it has a touch of sweet! Thank you, you worked hard."

"If you know, I start early, early in d' *mahn-in'.* You got to collect d' coconut fresh fo' d' day. I climb way up, mon. Yes, yes I do, to the top of d' coconut tree, *yezum*...I do. Thank you, thank you ma'am," he said, as Angie handed him the money, including a little extra.

Angie returned to find Ms. Rowena talking with three

other local women. Their beauty, in white and colored dresses and shade hats, and their loud, unrestrained laughter carried by the breeze made her pause to enjoy.

Once the introductions and exchange of Carnival pleasantries between Angie and the women were done, Ms. Rowena and Angie walked to the temporarily erected, slightly shanty, but colorful food booths in the Carnival Village.

"Miss Lillie makes a good meat *paté*."

"It's so pretty, and looks delicious," Angie said about the puffy, golden-fried, half-moon pasty.

"Over there, they got d' *salt fish, cassava, plantain*...and that booth, *stew fish and dumplin'*."

Angie watched Ms. Rowena beam while telling tales about the festive local foods.

With a preference for vegetables and food that she could identify, Angie was pleased to get a plate of *Callaloo*—leaves from the dasheen plant, cooked like spinach, and *fungi*—a thick slab of smooth, cooked cornmeal with okra pieces.

Ms. Rowena advised. "Take d' *johnnycake*."

Angie had declined the fried dough.

"Take it along, it's a journey cake," Ms. Rowena emphasized the morphed pronunciation, "to eat when you go."

Ms. Rowena explained in the laid-back island way of speaking, "*Johnnycake* will stick to you. It's a long day with the parade, y' know, and you—skin'n bones."

Because West Indian men like fleshy women, associated with fertility and sturdiness, Angie knew this comment was another nurturing gesture by Ms. Rowena.

The drum beat suddenly became staccato and thunderous, calling attention to the start of the parade. Cheers and whistles from the crowd showed their eagerness.

Ms. Rowena led Angie, from experience, to a spot of shade under a grand old tamarind tree. The elevated grassy area was just above the crowd, enough to catch the swirling trade winds—easterly winds that prevail in the tropics, formerly vital to the historic trade routes, and now to this area as a mecca for sailing.

Energy sparked in broad daylight as the leading floats presented the Carnival Queen, Prince and Princess.

Trinidad was the birthplace of the Caribbean Carnival. Of the various cultural influences in the Antillean island chain, those from Africa helped Carnival grow in vibrancy and meaning.

Colorful troupes of whirling costumed people and sequined dancers followed. The *fete* moved like an inchworm through the town street and around the park, which would make a long afternoon show.

As the festive musical sounds of the steel pan approached, a wave of people rhythmically moving in place, began. The steel pan band arrived on a flatbed truck and stalled in front of the tamarind tree.

The cheerful clinking and chinking instantly induced a carefree feeling, like being on vacation for Angie. She and Ms. Rowena swayed with the tunes—eyes closed as they mentally abandoned the here-and-now, for a while.

Most of this small "American Paradise," Virgin Island, was a national park. While still in her daze, Angie peeked across the expansive land views of undulating mountain sides with green trees and dry, brown, scrubby vegetation. She admired the silhouetted century plant stalks with yellow flower clusters reaching into the sky. She thought the surrounding electric blue and aqua Caribbean Sea made a stunning backdrop for the parade.

Reggae, soca, calypso…each band louder than the next. The Soca Boys' song, "…one cent, five cent, ten cent, dollar…" blared from the speakers mounted into the back of a jeep. The lively, suggestive rhythm got everyone gyrating their hips; left, right, back, forward, left, right, back, forward; then repetitively forward as the words changed to, "dollar, dollar, dollar, dollar…" The uninhibited movements raised giggles from Angie, while Ms. Rowena appeared serious about perfecting hers.

Everyone in the parade competed by color, sound, rhythm, and movement to be the flashiest. With feather masks to scanty costumes, the glitz and glamor was decadent.

"Where do they get these costumes?" Angie asked.

"I mek dem, some." The quivery mature woman's voice that answered was not Ms. Rowena's. Angie swiveled left and looked down in its direction. The voice came from beneath a broad-rim straw hat, completely covering whoever was underneath.

"You make some of these amazing costumes?" Angie asked.

"See, that's one." A spindly finger appeared, stretched beyond the hat rim, and pointed.

"Wow, oh my, so much time and detail!" Angie said of the strapless costume with a fitted, pearl and satin bodice, and fluffy taffeta and sparkle-tulle skirt.

Angie introduced herself by first name.

The voice under the straw hat replied. "I know, I know you is. I have d' sew shop on-island. You come by, I can sew d' button, d' hem, mek d' uniform right or mek a dress for you…anyt'ing, anyt'ing you need, Miss Nurse."

"Thank you, I will. I don't know how to sew; I'll be glad for your help. How should I call you?"

"Ms. Laullie. My shop is Laullie's Notions."

"I am very glad to meet you, Ms. Laullie. Happy Carnival."

"You too Miss Nurse, you too," Ms. Laullie said, with a momentary upward tip of the hat rim which revealed the slight-framed West Indian woman under it, seated in a beach chair.

Angie said, looking into the squinty brown eyes that smiled upward into hers, "There, now we know of each other. Thank you, Ms. Laullie."

The orangey-red flamboyant trees in bloom on the mountainsides looked vividly stunning to Angie, ignited by the warmth of meeting Ms. Laullie. Angie was becoming familiar with the hearts of the people, learning to *go easy*, *be as you are*, and that *we are one*. All reasons the nickname, Love City, was a good fit for this place in paradise.

"Genip!" A lean, dark-skinned man with waist-long hair in thick rope-like dreadlocks sang as he walked by carrying green-leafed branches with small round green fruits.

Ms. Rowena called, "*Okay,*" and shook two dollars in the air to trade for a bunch.

"Ah, Miss Angie, you got to taste dem, *mehson.* See...Do this."

Angie mimicked the demonstration, popping open the thin skinned, brittle casing with a slight squeeze between her front teeth. Next, she opened the hinged flap to one side, exposing the light pinkish-orange fleshy meat. With a pinch of the casing between her fingers, the succulent sphere launched into her open mouth.

"Good. Suck it, don't bite." Ms. Rowena instructed.

Tongue-rolling the smooth, moist, silky textured fruit-covered seed released a mouth-watering experience of mild, tangy-sweet flavor.

The bliss was brief; Angie wanted more.

She ejected the now bland, dehydrated, fur covered seed from her mouth. It was nearly the same size of the original fruit, lacking only the thin layer of delicious gel she had enjoyed.

"Now I see why you bought a bunch of them. Enough to last the rest of the afternoon."

The parade was a highly social event, attended by locals and visitors. Everyone was glad to be hanging out, island-style, called *limin'*. Ms. Rowena introduced Angie to many of the locals.

Angie watched the gentle, endearing, and playful yet direct manner Ms. Rowena had with people, and saw their respect for her. Her family, like most, came to Saint John as slave-captives from Africa, to work the Danish sugar plantations in the 1700s.

Ms. Rowena has wisdom about people and relationships. I am lucky to know her.

The noise and energy around them suddenly intensified. The stilt-walking *moko jumbies* enlivened the crowd.

"What are they? They're so tall," Angie said and

marveled at their balance and crazy antics.

"The moko jumbie is a friendly spirit, a healer. They are tall so they see ahead, into the future," Ms. Rowena said.

Clad with fire-engine-red, shiny satin costumes, masks or painted faces, hats and streamers, the moko jumbies turned and kicked up their long legs. The tallest of the five paused in place and walked his legs apart, then bent down to hand a giant daisy to a lady in the crowd.

A huge wheeled volcano by the Rotary slowly passed, with orange flames licking the crater opening at the top. Men and women club members scampered about and sang, "...I don't know where I'm gonna go, when the hurricane, she blow," to the melody of the Jimmy Buffett volcano song.

Following, the Girl Scout and Brownie float with the troops dancing 'round a campfire while singing, "It only takes a spark..." and "...down by the bay where the watermelons grow..."

Next in line, the high-stepping baton twirlers in gold sequined leotards, with giant lime foil sprigs and feathers in their headdresses, shimmied and marched to the drumbeat.

The yacht club's float sailed by. Under the flying Jolly Roger, a crusty, swashbuckling bunch of men on the makeshift deck singing "yo ho, yo, ho," floundered to hoist a white sail, while one stood peering through a spyglass.

"There's Jaco," Angie said.

In her few months on this little island of barely 3500 residents, she learned news and gossip travel rapidly by word-of-mouth, lightheartedly known as the *coconut telegraph*. Jaco was a hot topic among the expats girls— "good for a fun time," and "likes to dance," but "don't take him seriously."

He'd been on-island for years, from Scandinavia, never worked a job. Though debonair, he told about his life in tales of salty, sea faring ventures, portraying himself as a modern-day pirate. Many folks just rolled their eyes when his name came up.

The spyglass turned slowly, scanned the crowd, and then fixed upon her.

"Hey, Angie...Come to my yacht tonight for the show,

meet my dinghy at the dock before dark!"

"Okay, Miss Angie, you better go rest up for dem firecrackers," Ms. Rowena advised.

"I know not to take him seriously, but...he's safe to be around?"

"You go...have fun. I t'ink he's ok, if you don't get attached." Reflecting upon the lively time they shared today, Ms. Rowena added, "Ah, what a *spree* we've had, Miss Angie."

"Thank you, thank you, Ms. Rowena, for sharing this simply marvelous day."

Angie paused with anticipation. She wanted to give a hug, but wasn't certain about the etiquette. Ms. Rowena was the senior nurse at the health clinic. She hired Angie and seemed to have taken her under her wing.

They smiled at one another, and with a synchronized, slight forward head-bow, said, "*Okay!*"

Angie blinked away the moisture stinging her eyes—a mix of appreciation with a feeling of aliveness she wished would never end.

Each walked off in the direction of their home as the conch shell players sounded—the fanfare would continue for hours.

"Good show, Happy Carnival!" Angie greeted and waved to a resting moko jumbie seated atop a delivery-truck, with her flouncy multilayered skirt about her, and long decorated wooden legs reaching to the ground.

As Angie arrived at the end of town, the crowd thinned, the music and drums became more distant, and the road tilted uphill, winding toward home. The narrow, two-lane road had only a soft berm for its shoulder—no real accommodation for a pedestrian—the other side was against the rock face of the mountain.

She was not yet used to walking on these roads. Unlike 'in The States', here they drove on the left. She laughed at herself doing it again, like any recently transplanted person, comparing things to back home.

Just as Angie was feeling grateful for the *ez-doo* island attitude and slower pace of living, an open-air jeep full of loud hissing men, "sssss, sssss," flew past her right shoulder. It was the local way, instead of the stateside high pitch, followed by a low pitch whistle, to communicate a message of admiration.

That just doesn't feel the same ... slightly disrespectful ... hissing at someone, really ... They sound like a leaky spray can. Hmm, just something else to get used to. She shook her head and let it go.

Soon after arriving home, Angie snuggled comfortably into the body impression from the morning, still apparent in her mattress. She easily relaxed into sleep.

The sun was low in the sky when Angie came to. She wanted to linger in her bed to enjoy her deep satisfaction.

What a day! What a few weeks! No wonder people say, 'So much fun to have, no time to work.' With twenty-six or so holidays a year, having fun is a priority. Thank goodness I only have to work three days a week.

But she had to hurry to get ready for the fireworks.

As she parked her smiley-face-yellow jeep, Jaco pulled up to the dock, in a dinghy.

Like a giant magnet drawing her into the boat, "Good night, my lady, welcome aboard!"

Her heartbeat quickened. She let her breath go, noticed the calmness of the sea, and enjoyed the smooth dinghy ride.

Alongside his yacht, Jaco gestured for Angie to put her foot onto his lap. "May I?"

He removed her sandal, then the other, and added both to a pile against the dinghy's hull—presumably belonging to his other guests.

"Gotta protect the decks," he explained, pointing the way to board—a dangling rope ladder.

Her loose-fitting, mid-thigh length, sheer dress wafted as Angie climbed.

Glad I wore leggings.

What? Mouth and eyes, wide open. *He just grabbed my bum cheek!* Angie contained her reaction within her thoughts, but nearly blurted out something completely different.

"Lucky catch. Eh?" Jaco boasted.

Yeah, for who? Arcing her eyes sideways.

"Didn't want you to land in the water."

"I got this." She swung her leg over the gunwale and stepped onto the smooth teak deck.

There were a few other people on board. Jaco did introductions, gave her a tour and a fruity drink.

This feels like touristy-excursion hospitality...or is he doting on me?

"How long is your yacht?" A suggestive question that often challenges the ego of a male boat owner.

"Forty feet with the bowsprit. She's a classic wooden ketch, a fine lady to sail. We've harnessed lots of wind and covered many miles of sea together. I live on-board."

"Her name?"

"Mariah, my beloved from the sea."

Doesn't sound like there's much room for another gal in that relationship. But it's a cool bachelor pad— everything stowed, lines tidy.

The first of the fireworks brightened the dark night, and the brass hardware sparkled.

Folks on board scrambled to find their personal viewing space on the deck or in the cockpit.

Jaco led Angie to the bow of the boat.

"Best seat in the house!"

He assisted her with getting into the hammock-like net that hung from the bowsprit over the water—minding his hands better this time.

As he joined, the net sunk from his muscular weight, causing Angie to roll against his body.

Their spark was fun, but she wasn't ready to get burned.

Where's that fireman from J'ouvert to cool things off?

Suddenly fireworks crackled loudly above and sprayed color and light overhead as if to diffuse their heat. They startled into laughter and the embers rained down and faded out.

This final Carnival event was a dazzling orchestration

of fireworks with music. Under the popping, crackles, sparkling lights, and stars, Jaco held Angie while telling chivalrous pirate tales, and stories of the unfortunate island history of plunder, colonization and slavery.

Angie learned the Carnival on Saint John was a celebration of heritage and freedom—emancipation for their ancestors from Danish slavery on July 3rd, 1848; independence for their mother country, America, from the monarchy of Britain, on July 4th, 1776.

Feeling fancifully free, a subtle breeze played in her hair and carried her words into the night.

"Best Fourth of July ever!"

Barbara Young has travelled an interesting, less trodden path in life, which influences the perspectives in her writing. She was recently honored with the 2020 NCPA's Risk Taker Award for her story, *On the Porch with Miss Lizzy* in their 2019 anthology, *More Birds of a Feather*. In 2020 she introduced a precocious, wander-lustful and heart-driven nurse, who traveled through Europe with readers of the NCPA's 2020 *Destination: The World* anthologies. Angie continues her adventures in NCPA's *All Holidays, 2020* edition.

In 2018 Barbara's empowerment book for nurses, *The Heart that Rocks Health Care,* was published. She also creates poetry, children's stories, gift and coffee table books that feature her photography. Learn more at www.byoungbooks.com

Dear Carol,
Hope this story of your brief Island memories. Love ya, Soul Sistah!
Barbara

CHRISTMAS TREE HUNTING

SANDRA D. SIMMER

Our Christmas trees were usually purchased at a tree lot in town. But the year I was six, my teenage brother, Ted, suggested we cut down our own tree. We lived near several regional forests, so he argued that we could easily get a tree. My father, aka Daddy, remembered cutting down Christmas trees as a boy, and heartily agreed with the plan. My mother, aka Mama, was less enthusiastic, but didn't overrule the adventure. She just cautioned them to get a small tree to fit in the front window. Today it is highly illegal to cut down trees in the forest. But rules were more loosely followed, and rarely enforced at that time. As long as you weren't running an illegal logging company, rangers weren't upset by one missing tree. I begged to go along, so the three of us headed out Christmas tree hunting.

It was the middle of December 1961, on a mile-high plateau near the La Plata mountain range in southwest Colorado. Fields were covered with white crystalized drifts, and rooftops and trees carried a foot of snow. I was bundled up in thermal underwear, a long-sleeved shirt, corduroy pants, and my hooded winter coat. I also had cloth mittens to keep my hands warm. The last things I put on were wool socks, leather shoes, and my rubber overshoes on top. My pant legs were tucked into the top of the overshoes to help keep them dry. GORE-TEX or REI insulated clothing for middle-class consumers did not exist. Contemporary ski clothing was too expensive for my family. We set out in frigid weather in our layers of cotton and wool.

We did not have far to go. The pine tree forest on the ridge above McElmo Canyon was only three miles east of our house. My family collected pine nuts there in the fall, but I had never ventured into the forest in the winter. My father wasn't one to do extensive planning, so we simply took our family car on the trip. He threw a tarp and some rope in the trunk along with his ax, and proclaimed us ready to go. The well-used shovel and tire chains spent the winter in the car. Mama had prepared a thermos of hot chocolate while we were putting on our "snow clothes". We were only going to be gone an hour, so that was a pleasant surprise.

The county snow plow had come by the day before to clear the gravel roads that crisscrossed the countryside. Big piles of dirty brown snow lined either side of the roadway. The road itself proved easy traveling as we journeyed past our neighbors' farms. My friend Beth's house was at the end of the county road where the snow-plowed section ended. As we drove past her driveway, I imagined making her jealous with tales of my tree-hunting adventure. It seemed so exciting to pick our own special tree from the forest.

To reach the forest beyond the county road we had to drive on an un-cleared trail. Daddy wasn't daunted by a little snow. He had lived in it most of his life. He simply had Ted help him quickly put the snow chains on the tires. We were off-roading before long. There were wooden stakes poking out of the ground periodically to help mark the trail. But as we got a little farther into the forest the trees became thicker, and Daddy decided to stop.

Ted and I jumped out of the car and landed in piles of pristine drifted snow. The snow came almost to the top of my six-year-old knees. Cold moist snow immediately found its way into the top of my over shoes, but my bunched-up pant legs kept it from reaching my toes. I was used to walking in snow, so it did not bother me. Daddy and Ted strode ahead leaving tracks in the virgin snow pack. I hurried after them, hopping in and out of their footprints.

Finding a tree in a forest is not exactly as easy as it sounds. We were looking for a special tree; a Christmas tree. It had to be the right size, shape, and circumference. The perfect tree did not appear right away. We walked past one near the car that was a decent shape, but the branches were unevenly spaced and the top was bushy. Ted thought we could do better, so we pressed further into the forest.

We were three bears looking for the just-right tree. Some were too big, and some were too small, but none was just right. A tree would look good at a distance, but up close we could see its flaws. The three of us walked and walked, often circling back on our trail. The good thing about walking in snow is that you can't get lost. You can always follow your footsteps back to where you started, which is exactly what we ended up doing.

I got tired first and then cold. Trudging through the snow was exhausting, and when the snow worked its way down to my feet, I complained. Daddy immediately put me on his shoulders to carry me, but then he got tired as well. Only Ted still had enthusiasm for finding the perfect tree. When it started to snow my father said we had to leave. He thought the tree we first saw would be fine. Ted reluctantly agreed. Even he couldn't ignore the snow falling so thick it blurred the trail ahead.

When we got back to the car, Daddy started the engine to get the heater going. I was put inside with a cup of hot chocolate from the thermos. Daddy and Ted quickly set to work chopping down our Christmas tree. My excitement for the project returned as I eagerly watched them through the foggy front windshield. Daddy did most of the work wielding the ax, but Ted got in a few good whacks. Finally, the tree fell crashing into the snow in a cloud of icy spray.

Soon the tree was wrapped in the tarp and tied to the roof of the car. The new falling snow was filling in our tire tracks, and it wasn't possible to turn around in a snowbank. Daddy did a masterful job of backing the car out of the forest following our earlier tracks. Another half hour and he would've had a long hike to Beth's house to ask her father for a tractor tow.

When we arrived home, my mother met us at the door. She had been worried when it started to snow. Our quick one-hour trip had taken several hours. Daddy and Ted received a scolding for their crazy idea, which they ignored with good humor. I was put in dry warm clothes and sat by the pot-bellied stove to get warm.

My father and brother went back out to get the tree

before it became buried in snow. They shook off all the residual flakes at the back steps, and then triumphantly carried the tree into the living room. The tree was enormous! It had looked the right size next to bigger trees, but now dwarfed our living room. It was so tall they couldn't stand it upright. Mama gasped, Ted groaned, and Daddy and I laughed out loud.

They had to take it back outside and saw at least two feet off the bottom and make a wooden stand for the base. Daddy tried, without much luck, to fashion a point at the top to hold the Christmas angel. Nothing could be done to manage the branches in the middle that stuck far out into our narrow living room. You almost had to scoot around the tree when you walked past.

Mama was a good sport after her initial shock and concern. She retrieved boxes of Christmas lights and decorations from the attic. Ted strung the rows of primary colored tree lights. My teenage sister, Dana, got involved with decorating the tree with ornaments we had since her childhood. Daddy stood on a step-stool to duct tape the Christmas angel to one of the scraggly branches on top. Everyone participated in the final finishing touch. To imitate icicles, we covered the tree with long narrow strips of shiny silver tinsel; each one individually placed with care.

When we were done, we all stepped back to view our creation. It was the biggest, ugliest Christmas tree I had ever seen, and I loved it!

Sandra D. Simmer likes to write short stories and memoirs of her childhood adventures on her family's Southwest Colorado ranch. To enhance her skills, she is a member of two writing groups in the Bay Area. Sandra has short stories published in the NCPA's anthologies *Destination: the World* Volumes I & II, and is currently writing her first novel.

CHICKERY'S FIRST CHRISTMAS

NORMA JEAN THORNTON

The tree was up December One
It looked so nice when it was done

However, … by the following morn
From off the tree, things were tossed and torn

Thanks to Chickery, that little male kitten
And kitty-sis Curry, who was hissin; and spittin'

Up the tree they both climbed, all the way to the top
Not even once, on the way, did they bother to stop

As they ran up, Chickery unplugged every light
Ornaments flew off as they climbed, left and right

The garlands are hanging, down from the tree
Tangled in kittens, who are trying to get free

The branches are bowing, and look pretty tacky
Like a Charlie Brown tree, only worse, by cracky

How long can it stand, how long will it last?
Not long that's for sure; that tree's going quite fast

ENJOYING SUMMER CAMP HOLIDAYS

RONALD JAVOR

Right up there with the chicken-or-egg conundrum is the question, "Who has more fun at summer camp, the campers or the counselors?" The corollary to that eternal question is "Who *should* have more fun, the kids or the adults?" The answer is: all of them love to celebrate holidays!

Many years ago, I spent one summer as camp director at a rustic mountain camp with dozens of volunteer counselors. The camp provided multiple sessions, each attended by about 100 children from disadvantaged backgrounds living and playing together for ten-day periods. During those sessions, my job was to plan activities to keep everyone both happy and safe, so I often had to confront those two questions.

For most of the campers, it was their first time living in the mountains or even living away from home. They were together in small units, sleeping in rough lean-tos under the stars, with a counselor for each unit. The counselors were college students with, well, all the enthusiasm and creativity of young students. The campers didn't know any of the other campers before they arrived, and the counselors generally were strangers to each other as well. We needed family-building events to bridge those gaps and create a wholesome and enjoyable experience.

The camp had all the traditional activities—hiking, swimming, arts and crafts, and ballgames—but also had to fill some time each session with "special events" to keep the enthusiasm high for both sets of camp residents. Sometimes these activities were directly related to our outdoors location, such as focused nature walks and discussions about their surroundings. Other times we had all-camp contests like scavenger hunts or physical Olympics contests. But the most fun was when we celebrated "holidays": these events brought everyone together as an extended family to have fun together.

For the Fourth of July, we started our holiday preparations a day earlier. Campers each took one of their tee-shirts and either tie dyed, or decorated them with colored marking pens—or both—creating a variety of red, white and blue patterns or pictures. Counselors also made costumes for themselves, usually more intricate and creative but still using basic camp materials. Their Revolutionary War soldiers' costumes and weaponry made of tree limbs were works of art, patrician wigs made from mops were designed to remind us of George Washington or Benjamin Franklin, and Betsy Ross always seemed to show up sewing a flag. Each camper's unit and counselor also created a campfire skit or song, and practiced them during free time.

On the morning of July 4th, I rang the wake-up bell early. Overnight, camp staff and I had hung red, white, and blue paper streamers around the dining hall, on the doors, in the bathrooms and around the swimming pool fence. The campers walked by and under all our decorations and came to breakfast wearing their costumes, singing patriotic songs as they marched to the tempos sung by their units. The breakfast, and all meals that day, featured red, white, and blue food and drinks; they started by eating oatmeal with blueberries, fried sausage made as red as we could get it with red food coloring, and toasted white bread, all served with milk or juices, including tomato juice. All day long they marched together instead of randomly walking to their various activities, that were designed for that holiday: marksmanship with beanbag throwing, relay races with flags instead of batons, and 'hide-and-seek' as hidden soldiers. At campfire that night, each unit acted out its skit or performed its songs, and the counselors provided their own entertainment, a wacky skit spoofing me as an inept George Washington flailing with a small axe at a large tree.

Everyone, including the staff and me, were exhausted by bedtime!

Another favorite was on July 25 when we celebrated "Christmas in July." The campers spent extra time in the arts-and-crafts or nature programs making secret pal gifts for others. They made lanyards for neckwear—using up all the supplies of green and red materials—some decorated pine cones, or made wreaths with materials found around the camp. Each gift was numbered and each camper drew a number from Santa's bag as he or she arrived for dinner. All gifts were distributed during dessert.

Campfire after dinner featured Christmas carols and, of course, I made an appearance as Santa Claus because I came prepared with a Santa outfit. A number of counselors dressed as reindeer and elves, assisted in the rest of the celebration. Special sweet edibles were handed out to each camper as well as some special awards for those who were deemed "good" because they showed special care and attention to others during the preceding week.

One of my personal favorite camp holidays was celebrating the Perseid Meteor Showers in early to mid-August. We taught the campers how to make star charts in crafts during the day, and explained why the campers actually might see something special that night. At our altitude, far above the smog of Southern California, the stars didn't just twinkle, they shined brightly and virtually every moment would produce a bright falling star for them to wish upon. We predicted forty to fifty streaks each hour. After campfire and long after bedtime, we laid outside on the cold ground, covered with blankets and sleeping bags and watched meteors speed by and fall from the sky. The larger ones evoked cheers or "oohs" and "aahs". These sounds became less frequent, as the younger campers fell asleep, despite the cold.

The counselors ended the evening by suddenly appearing as "aliens" in a jerry-rigged walking UFO. These "aliens" demanded the campers take them to their leader. When the campers pointed me out, the "aliens" abducted me in their UFO with flashlight beams. The oldest boys' and girls' units then sang *"ET, Bring Our Leader Back"* to the tune of *"Michael Row Your Boat Ashore"* in order to rescue me before the "aliens" left Earth with me imprisoned in their UFO.

An important part of being at a camp in the mountains away from urban life was connecting more closely with nature. We achieved this with fun by borrowing from Native American lore. Native Americans believe that all living things are connected, that nature is our friend, and humans were created to take care of the Earth and its inhabitants. At least once each session we would have a day-long festival to celebrate the animals around us. Each unit would select an animal such as a bear, wolf, owl, deer, hawk, or buffalo and learn all they could about it. At the nightly campfire, each unit would celebrate its animal by telling the others about it and why it was important to humans, to other animals, or to nature as a whole. They might do this as a skit, as a made-up song, or just as a story.

In addition to our celebrations of these special holidays, we always had the most fun celebrating birthdays. Out of one hundred campers and two dozen counselors and staff, at least one birthday occurred during each session. On that special date, we would start the day singing "Happy Birthday" before breakfast to the lucky celebrant, and then arranged special favors and benign pranks throughout the day. Obviously, isolated as we were in the mountains without access to movie theaters, arcades, or restaurants, there were limits to what amusement we could provide for celebrations. But we could forgive chores, and allow the birthday boy or girl to visit the counselors' retreat room for a soda and snack.

At the nightly campfire, we continued each birthday celebration with skits, songs, and special treats. The counselors presented gifts to the lucky boy or girl whose birthday it was. Some of these could be useful items such as a camp tee-shirt or cap, but others would be gag gifts that had to be opened in front of everyone, like a real, or fake, dried deer poop paper weight with a birthday candle, or a collection of area insects arranged like a butterfly exhibit with funny names for each. I often wondered what the mothers and fathers thought when their sons or daughters brought home those gifts.

If we had no actual birthday during any ten-day session, or sometimes even in addition to an actual birthday, we would celebrate the birthday of a historical figure that the campers had heard of. For example, one night, on August 12, the staff and I worked frantically for hours after the campers went to sleep. Some counselors made and painted rough papier mache bats that were hung in entryways of each sleeping area, low enough to bump the campers' heads as they exited. Other staff used various materials to make weblike coverings in the doorways to the bathrooms and the toilet entries. A third group, including me, baked dozens of small, hard white flour balls and painted red splotches and large black dots on each, leaving them in the oven to dry and harden overnight.

The hubbub caused by the "webs" and "bats" as the campers walked to breakfast the next morning demonstrated their surprise and concern about these props. The noise level reached its crescendo after they saw the black crepe paper hung throughout the dining hall with various pagan symbols drawn on them as well as more bats and webs. The yelling and screaming then increased again to a complete uproar when oatmeal bowls were served with staring bloodshot white eyeballs in the hot cereal.

After breakfast, I explained we were celebrating Alfred Hitchcock's August 13 birthday. Most of the children had seen or heard of at least one of his scary movies. Our nature classes that day taught about the dangerous animals such as bats or bears around and above us, and how to avoid them. The day ended with the scariest campfire stories we could think of and those were augmented by our staff producing eerie sounds and thumps behind the campers in the darkness of the forest. I'm sure some of the campers may have taken awhile to get to sleep that night!

My favorite camper birthday was the celebration we held for 13-year-old Joey Green. Starting the first day of camp, he told everyone his birthday was coming up soon and he wanted a party. A couple of days before his birthday, for another camper's birthday, we had sung "Happy Birthday" at breakfast, excused her from daily chores, served a flat cake with candles at dinner and, of course, had birthday treats for her and the others at campfire. Given Joey's more aggressive and repeated expectations, we felt he deserved special treatment.

We decided to downplay Joey's birthday until breakfast was being served. I had planned with the kitchen staff to prepare a breakfast that would be special and unforgettable. After Joey woke up, he was disappointed his counselor didn't wish him happy birthday immediately and hadn't decorated his sleeping area. When he walked with his unit and the other campers to breakfast, there were no special decorations outside or inside the dining hall and his table had no special card or other recognition of his birthday.

After my usual pre-breakfast announcements, I told the campers that today was Joey Green's birthday, and for his present, he could lead the group in a song of his choice before breakfast. He looked disappointed but bravely walked up to the front next to me, recovered his swagger, announced his favorite song, and led the campers to begin singing.

While the loud strains of "*Rise and Shine*" and the accompanying clapping and foot stomping echoed through the rafters, I brought each unit's counselor into the kitchen. I had gotten out of bed at 4 that morning to work with the kitchen staff on a surprise: a special breakfast, to be served simultaneously, of green oatmeal, green-dyed scrambled eggs, toast spread with green butter, and green crepe paper napkins. When all the food-trays were placed on the table, the "euws," "yechs," and "ughs" almost drowned out the laughter. After a short grace, we sang "Happy Birthday" to Joey, and then most, but not all, of the campers hungrily dug in to eat the green food. Joey, of course, was thrilled and even asked for seconds.

We continued Joey's celebration at campfire. He sat by the fire on a "throne" covered with green shrubbery and was given an honorary camp tee-shirt dyed green. After another round of "Happy Birthday," we served the campers a light-green sheet cake; it was "light" because we had almost used up the entire kitchen's supply of green food coloring in the first meal and the cook refused to use arts-and-crafts green dye in food! Joey went to bed a very happy one-year-older boy with stories galore to share when he returned home.

I always found it amazing that early in each camp session, the campers and counselors were utter strangers but then quickly morphed that relationship from children to take care of, into little brothers and sisters. Many of the campers who were shy to begin with blossomed as they shared holidays together. Even the counselors quickly became extended family with each other, and these holidays were all completely different than any I ever had with my own family. They were just as meaningful, and often even more fun, than the more traditional holidays I enjoyed at home, and in the end, we all became an extended family!

Ronald Javor lives in Sacramento and spent his legal career assisting people with low incomes, disabilities and homelessness to access safe and affordable housing. He has written seven children's books on young people confronting and overcoming these barriers. Each book addresses negative stereotypes and shows that all children, despite their handicaps, have the same goals and desires. More information is available on the books at ronaldjavorbooks.com.

Since "retirement", Ron volunteers his time continuing the same work as well as advocating for environmental justice. He also continues his writing interspersed with travel and camping. His pendng Young Adult book, *Our Forever Home*, features Lonesome George, the extinct Galapagos tortoise, and Dodo, an extinct bird, exploring the past and present worlds of extinct animals, the effects of climate change, and what can be done about them to save today's animals, including humans.

'TWAS

ROSEMARY COVINGTON MORGAN

December 24, 1954

Cynthia won't be quiet. She is never quiet. Always running, jumping, rolling across the floor. To this day, she has an energy I can only wish to have. Tonight, she is jumping on the bed singing the only words of the only Christmas carol she knows, "Jingle bells, jingle bells, jingle all the way."

The same words, over and over and over. To the rhythm of her singing, she jumps once on her feet, then bounces on her butt and repeats over and over and over. The box springs under the mattress squeak like an animal in pain trying to sing along. I want to scream, but can't because Santa might hear, so I whisper, "Please, please be quiet," begging to no avail, near tears with frustration.

I am 5 and Cynthia is 2. She does not yet know that her elder should be obeyed! So, I pull the covers over my head. The room is dark. If Santa appears, he might not notice I'm here.

My sister and I are upstairs in the bedroom of our large, old three-story house. Normally, only guests sleep up here. We were sent upstairs because Santa will be downstairs shortly and all children must be asleep when he comes. We should be asleep by now.

Except for Cynthia, it is spooky quiet. Even our baby brother, who usually keeps our parents up all night, is downstairs sleeping. We seldom come up here. It's very scary and I'm sure there are ghosts. But it's Christmas Eve and Mother and Daddy thought we would go to sleep faster if we were upstairs.

Finally, Cynthia stops jumping and snuggles next to me to sing in my ear. She will grow up to have a beautiful singing voice, but not yet. Right now, it's just kind of a screech.

I am just about to put my hands over my ears, when we hear it – the sound of heavy footsteps on the stairs. **BOOM,** one step; **BOOM,** two steps; **BOOM** the next, like little bursts of thunder, getting louder with each step. The **BOOMs** are nearer. *On no, it's Santa.* Cynthia stops singing and looks at me. We are both frightened. Santa has heard us! He's coming to put coal over our bed. No toys for us.

The footsteps are on the landing now, echoing down the long hall. We are still awake; *Santa will cover us with coal dust!* Cynthia starts to cry loud sobs, making things worse. I pull Cynthia further under the covers and rub her back so she will stop crying. It doesn't work.

Through the blankets, I can see the door open and the hall light glow on a large shadow in the doorway holding something in his hand. *Maybe it's not Santa, maybe it's a ghost!* I am too scared to move. Now, tears are beginning to seep from my eyes. The shadow is coming toward the bed. I hold my body tight and still, waiting for the coal to be thrown on the bed or the ghost to take us away.

The figure pulls the covers off us. I hold on to my blanket, squeezing my eyes closed, pretending to be asleep. Cynthia jumps up, giggling with glee. I open my eyes. It's Daddy. He's carrying a book.

With a big smile on his handsome face, he sits on the side of the bed and begins to read in his sweet baritone voice: *'Twas the night before Christmas…*

By the time the parents in the book had *settled down for a long winter's nap,* Cynthia was asleep. But I'll never forget Daddy almost singing as I drifted into dreamland: *Now Dasher! Now Dancer! Now Prancer and Vixen! On Comet! On Cupid! On Donder and Blitzen! To the top of the porch! To the top of the wall! Now dash away, dash away, dash away…*

For Cynthia

RoseMary Covington just stepped on stage for an encore. After a 40-plus-year successful career as an urban planner, her curtain rises on a new challenge as an author.

Writing isn't new to her. Born in St. Louis, Missouri, she created stories using her dolls and plastic action figures in elementary school. Her interest followed through high school, to the University of Missouri- Columbus and Washington University-St. Louis.

Her early career included investigating civil rights cases, housing development, reviewing grants, and developing community-based programs. She began the development of major public transit projects, becoming an executive manager and acknowledged expert in her field.

She has led transit projects in St. Louis, Cleveland, Washington, DC, Sacramento, and other cities as a consultant.

RoseMary has published short stories, *The Song* in the *Storytellers-Tales from the Rio Vista Writers' group* anthology plus *My Big Red Shadow, and School Shopping* in NCPA's 2020 Travel Anthologies *Volumes-1 and 2.*

FINDING MY WAY HOME

SANDRA D. SIMMER

The North Star shines bright in the December sky.
It guides my footsteps down the frozen lane.
As I struggle to move through the knee high drifts,
countless snow crystals crunch beneath my boots.

I manage to maintain my balance though
my arms are piled high with packages
wrapped in brightly colored paper, tied 'round
with ribbons made rigid by the cold.

My breath freezes in the cold night air;
puffs of exhaled fog surround my face.
As it begins to snow, I see, through the mist,
the Christmas tree lights shining in the window.

I am home at last!

CROSS-CULTURAL RING OF LIFE
KIMBERLY A. EDWARDS

On February, 11, 1970, I attended a new-student party in a private home at the California college I was entering. The program was unique: small, only 250 students, half from Latin America, half from the U.S. Coursework was delivered in Spanish. Since I knew the language from high school classes and homestays in Mexico, I considered myself familiar with culture south of the border. Little did I know, as I would come to learn.

Students from Latin America arrived at the college glassy-eyed after a long flight to a strange land. They responded differently to culture shock, more than I could understand at age eighteen. Disorientation lasted days or in some cases weeks, though the signs were not always evident. The majority were male, largely from Central and South America. I spent most of the evening at the new-student party talking with someone I'll call Mauricio. I'll disguise his country as well, but let's say it lies below the equator in South America.

He was tall and thin, rather lanky, with a headful of curly brown hair and a silver chain around his neck. His last name was not a recognizable Hispanic name, but this was not unusual, as immigrants from Italy, Germany, and other European countries flooded South America following World War II. I don't remember our conversation, but we laughed in that new-student glow. As the chairs filled up, we slid down to the carpet, soft and soothing to insecure students in a new environment. Time fell away, helped by the spiked punch and the music of Santana and romantic composer Armando Manzanero. By the end of the night, Mauricio and I gave each other pet names. Mine was "Little Lamb." It was all a joke, and we parted as friends.

Over the next few days, my world exploded in a

whirlwind of experiences: dorm living, textbooks in Spanish, and a welcoming family of classmates from all over the Americas. Flags for every Latin American country reigned over the student lounge. We ate meals in our special dining hall, symbolizing the private bubble we inhabited within the larger English-speaking university. On Saturday nights, our student lounge rocked with twirling, hip-shaking cumbia dances. Sundays brought spirited soccer games played between fellow classmates on teams from the U.S., Mexico, Central America, and South America.

Romances or rumors of romances permeated daily living. Most relationships occurred between males from Latin America and females from the U.S. These liaisons, as I would learn, bred misunderstandings, exacerbated by youthfulness and differing backgrounds, expectations, primary language, and cultural practices. We were an experiment in intra-American living and we basked in this identity.

Three days after the new-student party, on Valentine's Day, Mauricio the guy from the party approached me as I was leaving the dining hall.

"I have something for you," he said, digging into his pocket. I had forgotten how tall he was. Fellow students passed as they exited the lunchroom, bringing the scent of chocolate ice cream cones with them.

"For me?" I asked, somewhat puzzled.

He held out a box, professionally wrapped. "For Valentine's Day," he said.

I was more conscious of the students filing past than of Mauricio holding out a present. No guy had ever given me a gift for Valentine's Day, much less a guy I didn't know and didn't plan to claim as a boyfriend.

"You can read the card, if you like," he said.

Tucked under the bow lay a note with a message handwritten in ink: "*To little Lamb, Let's see what the future holds...*"

Shifting from foot to foot, I hemmed and hawed as long as I could. Most of the students had passed. We were alone. When my delay became obvious, I untied the bow.

As I pulled back the wrapping, a jeweler's box appeared. Alarm bells went off in my head. I felt a flush pass over my cheeks. Hesitant, embarrassed, maybe a little afraid, I lifted the hinged lid. Inside, a ring, a piece of costume jewelry with a round orange stone.

To say that I was shocked would be an understatement. I was horrified. A girl didn't get a ring from a guy unless the couple were going steady or getting married. A gasp must have escaped me, as Mauricio looked startled. Confusion filled his face.

"I-I'm not sure what to do with this," I said, snapping the lid closed. I don't remember if I spoke in English or Spanish.

"I don't understand," he replied.

Doesn't matter if you understand, I cried to my mortified self. Somehow, I uttered a thank you, pushed the box in my purse, and excused myself. Scurrying to my dorm, I wasn't sure if I should scream or hide my face.

At the dorm, the account of the gift spilled out before I could put the words in order. The girls all roared with laughter as they passed the little box from hand to hand. How could a guy do such a dumb thing after just three days?

Knowing how fast tales spread, I envisioned the story swirling down the dorm hall, rising to the upper floors, exiting the windows, and sweeping over the lawn to the two men's dorms. The tale would circle the tables at mealtimes. I pictured heads lowered in whispers in the back row of classrooms.

By now I knew I wanted nothing to do with Mauricio. As far as I was concerned, he was non-existent for having committed a great blunder. When I passed him in the hallways, I kept my gaze straight. At meals I sat at a table far away

A week later, a knock on my door alerted me to a phone call on the dorm phone. I pressed down the collar of my blouse. Maybe someone was going to ask me for a date. I ran to the phone, halfway down the hall.

"Hello?" I said in the nicest voice I could muster. A pause signaled that the caller was someone in the early stage of English language learning.

"Good night," came the words, slowly formed. Mauricio! His teacher had forgotten to tell him that in English, *Buenas noches* can mean Good night or Good evening.

"Good night," he repeated. "Would you like to go to the dining hall for dinner?"

"I'm going with friends," I said, disappointed that no one was calling me for a date.

"Tomorrow?"

"Busy."

A few days later, this scene repeated itself. I turned him down again.

The third time he called, I couldn't contain my exasperation.

"Good night," he greeted when I answered the phone.

"Good night!" I replied, slamming down the phone. I returned to my room to get ready for dinner with the girls again.

That was the last time he called.

Unfortunately, that was not the end of Mauricio. He hovered in my thoughts, as I kept him in my peripheral vision, making sure to steer clear of him at all times. I treated him as if he were radioactive. If he stood on one side of the room, I moved to the other. Thankfully, he must have sensed my hostility, as he honored the distance.

One lonely Saturday night several months later when a few friends found ourselves bored, we scaled the chain-link fence surrounding the university pool. We all jumped in and treaded water in our clothes, enjoying the act of breaking campus rules. I saw that Mauricio was part of the group. No words were spoken, but we shared a coincidental laugh as we moved our limbs silently to stay above water while not alerting campus police. My disdain softened, but only a little.

Eventually Mauricio got a girlfriend. In fact, he had a few. One of my girlfriends went out with him every time he called. Not long after graduation, he married one of our fellow students, a very sweet girl. Unfortunately, as I would later hear, the marriage didn't last.

Over the next few years, I got married and stayed busy

raising three kids. Mauricio retreated into the distant past except as an oddity in an old college story, which by now I could relate with amusement.

In the early 1990s, when my youngest child was in second grade, I thumbed through his yearbook, noticing a boy who had Mauricio's last name. Could it be...? Couldn't be. Could it be? No, couldn't be. But those thoughts carried me back to that faraway incident and my reaction. Had I been too mean to Mauricio by outright rejecting him?

In approximately 2006, at a college reunion, I saw photos of our school soccer teams, and there was Mauricio. A twinge of nostalgia passed through me, the curly brown hair, slim physique, young face of promise. But quickly I realized that my longing was not for him, but for the young girl who had arrived at college with many dreams and with her life ahead of her.

With the Internet becoming popular, our college classmates began to stay in touch regularly. Many had gone on to interesting professions: managing international companies, teaching English or directing educational programs, serving in high government positions in their home countries. The face of my former fellow student with brown hair and the unusual last name came to me only now and then. I wondered what he had become, but the curiosity never lasted longer than a minute. Still, I asked myself why I was so repulsed. Couldn't I have just told him what a ring meant in my culture? Ask him what it meant in his culture? Show courtesy, be a friend, tell him I didn't like him romantically?

In 2011, my college held a reunion in Quito, capital of Ecuador. I looked forward to going. Time had convinced me of the deep ties with former classmates. I wondered if Mauricio might attend. What would I say to him? I was beginning to feel guilty. Would I have the courage to apologize?

Quito sits at the foothills of the Andes. I checked into my room. The scent of nearby Eucalyptus trees slid through the open window. I changed my clothes twice for the opening reception. Why did I keep wringing my hands? Yes,

Mauricio had done something stupid. He was naive. He violated local customs. I, in turn, oblivious to his new status in the country, was too immature to respond other than to rebuff him publicly.

I took the elevator down to the salon where the reunion would take place. The twinkling lights around Quito were just coming on. There at the check-in table stood Mauricio. He was dressed in a beige suit and tie. He was as tall as before and his hair was still brown.

At once I approached him. Without any preamble or formalities, I spoke in English. "I am sorry that I was not nice when you gave me a present years ago."

He cracked a smile and raised a palm to signal that he was just as eager to unload his own burden. "It was my fault," he admitted. His English was better than my Spanish after my many years of not using the language consistently.

I noted that he didn't exactly look me in the eye, nor did I in his, but communication seemed to come from a deeper place.

"I wasn't thinking straight," he said. "My roommates told me the custom for Valentine's Day was to buy a gift for a girl you like. What a fool I was."

Whatever his explanation, just like that I accepted it and just like that, 40 years of acrimony vanished.

Now that we made peace, I told Mauricio of the coincidence of the boy in my son's class years earlier who had the same last name. He would now be 26. Mauricio said that yes, he had a son, born to a woman he had married, now living in my city. The marriage, his second, didn't work out. He returned to his country. He hadn't seen the boy for years due to a bitter divorce and U.S. visa restrictions following September 11. Remarkably, we concluded that this was Mauricio's son in my own boy's class. That night, as the city twinkled around us and the scent of Eucalyptus slipped through an open window, we with a group of classmates sat in the bar on the top floor of the hotel, drinking and singing to the music of Manzanero.

After the reunion, Mauricio and I emailed occasionally. He complained about the child's mother, who wouldn't allow

191

the son to visit Mauricio in his country. I counseled him on trying to build a relationship with his son, his only child.

In 2013, word came via our college email system that Mauricio's son had died of an overreaction to a drug. I couldn't think of anything crueler than to lose an only child. I emailed Mauricio. He could not get a visa in time to attend his son's memorial service. He did not even have a photo of him.

As if the boy were my own child, I set out to obtain photos of him. It seemed like the least I could do. I contacted the schools our sons attended. Some of the counselors remembered me, but the principals didn't want to oblige me because I wasn't the parent. This didn't stop me; I pressed on. Eventually I received a few photocopies, which I sent to Mauricio. He expressed deep appreciation.

In 2015, another reunion was planned. I looked forward to seeing Mauricio. There was freedom in our invisible new union, having made errors as youth and having come to our senses as adults. The first event was a luncheon. He was already seated when I arrived. He came over to the meal line. We hugged. The barrier that had existed for 40-plus years was gone.

"How are you?" I asked.

"I got married," he said. "My new wife is here. I'd like to introduce her to you."

In some strange way I felt like a sister whose approval mattered. Our relationship, as I would later figure out, had transformed. I was happy to meet his new wife, his third.

Four years later, in 2019, another reunion took place in California. I knew that Mauricio wouldn't be attending, but I looked forward to seeing everyone else.

The first activity was a backyard event in a private home. When I arrived and was pouring a drink, one of Mauricio's countrymen came over to me. We were alone. After the usual embrace and niceties, he said, "We've received some bad news."

"Oh no," I said, unable to imagine what he planned to say, since I was not a close friend.

"Two weeks ago, one of our classmates died."

"What?"

"Mauricio."

A shadow fell over the table on which my glass sat, but I managed to finish pouring my drink, "No," I said.

"A massive heart attack. His brother emailed me last week."

"And his wife?" I asked, biding me time to process this terrible news.

"No, they divorced. Divorced a few years ago."

Three wives, I thought. I wondered if he was alone when he died.

After expressing the expected sorrow, I joined a table where my closest friends sat. As conversation went on around me, I felt the dull pain of absence, a void to be acknowledged. I saw Mauricio holding out a wrapped Valentine's gift. I heard his painstaking attempts to say good night when he meant good evening. I felt the warm water the night we swam in the college pool in our clothes.

Most of all, I caught the scent of the Eucalyptus trees that blew through the window as we shared a healing minute in Quito. That exchange gave me joy and relief. As strange as it sounds, I really didn't know Mauricio well as a person, nor he, me. But we had experienced each other's foibles, bare and bad, in our journey from young to mature. Nothing would take that intimate glimpse away. I realized that the ring of life is more universal than cultural. The bond I felt to Mauricio started with an unwanted ring on Valentine's Day.

Kimberly A. Edwards loves writing about curious things, including inequities, she observes along life's path. These subjects offer levels of interpretation that take her years to figure out, and even then she continues revising to illuminate new discoveries. Her travel often serves as the backdrop for stories. Marginalized communities and the lessons they have taught her appear in many of her pieces. For decades she has written articles, but literary nonfiction is her favorite genre. Kim recently finalized her book for the History Press on early Sacramento motorcycling in the first half of the 20th Century. She is an alumnus of Squaw Valley Community of Writing (Fiction), and the Kenyon Review Writer's Workshop (Non-fiction and Hybrid). A long-time NCPA member, she also serves as president of the local branch of the California Writers Club.

POPPET'S HAIRSTYLE:
A CHRISTMAS TAIL
ROBERTA DAVIS NARRATED BY NACHT

"Tell us a fireplace story, Uncle Nacht."

The request came from one of the foster kittens. Nacht lifted his head from where he lay stretched out near a crackling fire in an old hearth of large stones. His long fur wasn't half as thick as it used to be this time of year, but he didn't need to grow such a thick winter coat anymore. His once dull, black fur now shone in the firelight. Silver speckled his coat at an early age from a rough start, something these kittens might avoid. *Brats,* he thought, *but they're cute, and better than wildlife of all kinds trying to steal my dinner.*

He often had flashbacks to life on the street, but for now, life was good. His human, Celeste, had the habit of inviting little cats to share the abode. This time they had five guests, all around four-weeks old, named Snowy, Tibblez, Lunarpaws, Raggletag, and Butterfluff. The kittens would grow, get fat and sassy, and leave with different humans.

Celeste watched them for brief moments between her tasks of putting wooden ornaments on a tree, scribbling on cards, and fastening jubilant paper around boxes. Boxes! She left some open, which the kittens took great delight in tumbling around in, as they wrestled and scampered about.

Nacht wondered if they'd ever tire out. They seemed to, but not for long. After zooming through the house a few more times, the five kittens surrounded him, a usual encounter where they swatted at his feet, ears, and tail, energetic and insistent. Usually they wanted play time. Tonight, a storm was brewing outside, and they needed after-dinner comfort.

"Tell us a story," Raggletag instigated.

The others chimed in, using their cutest, needy voices. He knew they wouldn't stop any time soon.

"Okay, okay," Nacht sighed, rising. Maybe he could entice them even further into a food-induced sleep. He dragged a bag of treats off the table, sauntered back to the fireplace, and ripped the bag open. He let the little furballs dig in, a show of insatiability.

"Now, this is a crazy story the cat outside told me. She just got back from being abducted by our Celeste, of all people!"

"Why would she do that?" piped a runty calico with bright orange amongst her brown and black markings.

"She takes us to doctors, Butterfluff," Nacht replied.

The kittens started to bombard him with questions, about cages, pokes and prods by humans, and being taken to strange, scary places. Nacht waved them off and set his paws down on the treat bag. "You want these? Then let me tell the story." That worked. He sat down near the fire's warmth with the kittens before him, a few of them batting at each other.

"This story is about a feral cat named Poppet."

A black kitten with a white nose and feet snickered, "What kind of dumb name is that?"

"It's a British term for sweetie. You see, Tibblez, Poppet's been mooching dinner, as strays do. She finally let a few humans pet her. She sleeps in either their garage, or a boat."

"How come she doesn't use one of the little houses outside? Celeste said they're for cats," said Snowy. She was snowy looking, with random dark grey spots like shadows. Beside her, the two tabbies started wrestling. Within seconds, the kittens were arguing over 'he-touched-me' and 'she-ate-my-treat'.

"Quit it," Nacht said before a five-way scrap commenced. He grabbed the bag and shook out more treats, ensnaring their attention once more. "She does. The cats here just don't accept her too well, so she eats and runs. One day, the neighbors started talking about Poppet. Is she feral or tame? Nobody knew because Poppet acts like she's scared of most, but nice to a few people. One gal said Poppet's family either left without her, or lost her."

They all watched as their cat lady walked by in comfy clothes and a big jacket, carrying lots of cat food. She even took a kettle of warm water with her out into the cold. Gloomy clouds threatened with rain, while hanging strings of lights shimmered like multi-colored fireflies. Cats gathered outside, along with one mouthy cat, a mess of long fur.

"That's Poppet, the chatterbox," Nacht said with a smirk. "You remember hearing some awful squalling the other night? That was Poppet. It's been freezing at night. I know by the morning frost. Celeste was saying Poppet sounded sick and she was gonna take her to the doc. They could do a chip scan and maybe learn who this cat is. So, Celeste grabbed Poppet and took her for a jaunt into town. Boy, that didn't go over very well. Poppet cussed so loud, all the other cats ran away from their dinners and had to finish eating later."

"Poor Poppet," Snowy said.

"Oh, it got juicier. When they went in the doc's office, Poppet shot out of the carrier and went tearing through the place. Humans were scampering after her like dogs chasing a car. One went after her with a carrier that could fit a huge rodent. Celeste yelled at that person. Nobody was at their best that night. Poppet was a flying furball and led them on a merry chase. She thought she'd eluded the humans and could sneak out, once they started eating doughnuts." He leaned toward the kittens, making the fire's light cast a scary shadow of him as he stomped toward the kittens. As they stared up at him, he exclaimed, "And then, then she saw a big towel lumbering toward her with legs and fingers. Not the towel trick! They caught her again." He sighed and sat back down. "Poppet didn't say much after that except there were cages and strange people carrying her around, and oh, how she hates to be carried!"

"That's awful," the grey tabby whined before smacking her brownish brother.

"Well, that too, passes. You'll have to see the doc too.

You'll get over it. So then, she went to another place called the SPCA. Been there." He frowned, not wanting to reminisce, nor scare the kittens. "Living here is much better. More people debated over Poppet and stuck her in a different cage. All the time, Poppet was complaining and saying 'Lemme out, it's me, it's me!' but the humans didn't understand her. Not even Celeste was there, which is very odd."

The brown tabby looked up with big eyes. "Why would Celeste abandon her? Is that gonna happen to us?"

Nacht paused, his whiskers twitching in thought. "Sometimes there's overnight stays. So, here's what happened. Poppet said, a few days after she went to uh, the doc, Celeste got to talking to some invisible folks in that gadget she's always on and made a huge fuss. She was blurting, 'Holy Crap, that's my cat?!' She ranted on about a chip and long-lost feral and she had to get the cat out of there pronto. She gave this long explanation that she had Poppet fixed and then Poppet vanished soon afterward. Celeste didn't see her for a long time, whole seasons. Over that time, Poppet must have changed color so much that nobody recognized her, not even Celeste. Then last year, a new cat showed up and Celeste started feeding the mystery cat."

"Who was the mystery cat?" asked Butterfluff.

Nacht clarified, "It was Poppet the whole time! Like I said, her coat got darker, and a fat, dark stripe ran down her back. All this time, humans thought it was a different cat."

The kittens looked at each other, Lunarpaws and Tibblez uttering "Oooh," while the other three rummaged for the last scattered treats.

Nacht went on, "Poppet said she didn't understand why a cat can't get a new hair color when humans do it all the time and nobody captures them for it. She was furious over the whole thing. How dare those stupid humans shuffle her around! How indeed. How could Celeste not recognize her? Well, I'll tell you how. Humans can't smell as good as we can. They're not as evolved as we are. That chip sure was a big deal, though. Celeste cussed and told a long story to the invisible friends inside her gadget. Then she lost her keys, found them, went looking for her phone, and couldn't find one shoe. It was quite a show. All the while she was grumbling about a stupid microchip that her expensive scanner didn't read right. Mad, mad!"

"I heard it," Snowy said. "We were hiding. Wait, what's a chip?"

"I'm not sure," Nacht admitted. "I thought chips are food. Celeste was saying 'that damn chip, freaking cat,' while she did that thing where she walks in circles, cussing." He and the kittens shared a laugh. "She said Poppet no doubt ran off after getting spayed. Well, who wouldn't wanna run off?"

"What's spayed?" Tibblez asked.

"Oh, uh, I'll tell you when you're older," Nacht evaded.

"It's so you can't make babies," Butterfluff whispered.

"Where'd you hear that?" Lunarpaws chided.

"It's true," Nacht said before they could start arguing. "Do you wanna make little kittens? Play house?"

Raggie laid his ears back. "Ew. No way. I wanna hunt mice and eat worms, like wild cats do."

"Believe me, it's overrated … and don't talk to strange Toms. They're not all as cool as me. Moving on," Nacht said, "so while Poppet was gone, she changed so much that no human recognized her. Celeste was really embarrassed because she knows us cats better than humans. Poppet showed up and after some months, she started talking to Celeste, rubs on her and enjoys getting petted. Celeste kept complaining about the cat being feral like it was a big surprise. She told a long story about the cat being caught and fixed years ago, and then soon after, Poppet vanished. We were stunned to learn the new cat was her long-lost Poppet, mooching food as if nothing happened. Well, of course, our human had to have the cat back because people don't want to adopt a feral cat—because well, humans are human. They usually only want ferals if we'll eat their giant rats that have jagged teeth and big, nasty claws, and long tails like snakes." He chuckled as the kittens shrank back. "Oh, you'll grow bigger than most vermin."

Lunarpaws shrunk behind the other kittens as she muttered, "Most vermin? I'll stick with chicken, thanks."

Snowy head-butted Raggletag. "There's your mouse burgers."

"Not if I gotta live outside," Raggletag hissed. "There's scary crap out there!"

Nacht cleared his throat, redirecting their attention for the umpteenth time. "So anyway, our human took off in a flurry and later that day, brought Poppet home."

Tibblez gazed around, "So where's Poppet?"

"Weren't you lissening? She's outside," Butterfluff answered.

"Why?" Snowy piped.

"Coz," Nacht sighed, "not every cat figures out it's okay in here. And humans, well, it's complicated. But one thing's for sure, that cat was sure happy to get the heck out of human's houses, and the humans at the SPCA were very happy to give her back to Celeste. Then Poppet cussed out Celeste and took off."

"Poppet's a drama queen," Butterfluff snickered. "I think they both are."

"Yeah, but ours takes good care of us," Nacht replied, with a toothy grin. He stretched out on the rug and rolled onto his back, rubbing his full belly with his big paws.

"But what happened to Poppet? She's not gonna live out there," Lunarpaws said, her whiskers drooping. "Forever?"

"For now, that's where she feels safer," Nacht said in his stoic wisdom. "Eh, you never know. She only cold-shouldered Celeste for one day before being buddies again. Shh, hear that?"

The kittens hushed, a short-lived silence. Outside, in the breezy, cold night was the happy voice of Celeste, the muffled sounds of soft cat kibble, crunching sounds from a few other ferals chowing down, and the plaintive meows from Poppet.

"Poppet's home just in time for holiday leftovers. Happy Catmas to all, and to all a good cat: Merry Christmas, kiddos," Nacht said with a yawn.

 Roberta "Bert" Davis, pen name "Berta D," has written sci-fi/fan since childhood. She served in the Air Force Reserves, 940th Air Refueling Wing as MSgt, with twenty years as a crew chief on the KC-135 aircraft and two years as Wing Historian. She now works as a tech writer/design artist. Bert graduated from Embry-Riddle Aeronautical University with a dual MS in Aeronautical Science.

Her time is largely spent supporting animal rescue, including wildlife. Roberta is working on a series starring cats. She has done TNR or rescue for years, helps get strays indoor homes, and cares for a small colony of feral cats. Bert has four ex-feral cats inside, named Raggle Taggle, Luna Lovepaw, Mr. Tibbles, and Hufflepoof "Poofy."

Roberta is published in multiple anthologies, two from SSWC, and several cat stories in NCPA anthologies. Her sci-fi novel, more of a life's work, is in contract to be published.

HOLIDAY PRESENTS

ROSEMARY COVINGTON MORGAN

They are the days for
Older Ones
Younger Ones and
Those in between

Hot Dogs
Turkey
Steaks and Ice cream

Fruit Pies
Birthday Cakes
Puddings, peppermint

Singing
Laughter
Dancing and games.

Trees
Lights
Fireworks and flags

I guess those things still exist
Contagious with wonder
Pleasure and enjoyment.

The world I'm sure
Will stop for a day
To express itself
With reverence and playfulness.

Yet every year we
Face our holidays
With a little less cheerfulness
And a bit more fear

Pausing
In the midst of celebration
Knowing
Someone's not here.

TOMBOY TALES:
THE CHRISTMAS SURPRISE

BARBARA A. BARRETT

The events in "The Christmas Surprise" are based on the adventures of two tomboy sisters who were fortunate enough to live in a small town in Wisconsin in the 1940s.

I belly-flopped on my sled and went over the edge of the ravine. The speed and the wind in my face took my breath away. Packard Hill was really fast today; cleaning my sled runners with steel wool worked. My sister, Jeanie, was a few feet away. Her sled was as fast as mine. The hill sloped into the ground below and we were down. I steered away from her and stopped.

Jeanie spoke first, "Wow! That was fast!"

I looked down the long ravine. The other side seemed miles away. I just wanted to glide until the sled stopped. "Yeah, I bet we could have gone a mile. Too bad it's such a long walk back."

"Let's go again."

I nodded and grabbed the rope, dragging my sled. The wood was worn and I could barely see the red arrow in the middle. The new sleds had red runners, and on the shiny wood, the *Flexible Flyer Arrow* was clear and bright. I sighed. My sled was fast but I had to bend my legs backwards so they'd fit.

The snow crunched beneath my feet as I climbed. It was steep and our clothes were wet and heavy. At the top, I picked up my sled and ran toward the edge, flopping down on my stomach a few feet before I went over. It was like flying. Nothing between me and the bottom, and it didn't take long to get there. What we really needed in this town was a slanting hill that went for miles.

Jeanie steered until she was next to me. We trudged back up the hill. Again, it was slow going with lots of time to think.

"Grandma and Pappy will be here next week for Christmas." It's difficult to jump up and down wearing heavy snow suits but Jeanie managed it on the hillside. I admired her balance and waited for the inevitable question whenever our grandparents were coming.

"What are we going to do for them?" Jeanie asked. Usually, we dressed in costumes and acted out a song.

I shrugged, "It's going to have to be outside."

She nodded. We both knew Mom was getting ready for Christmas. Today, she was washing the bedding and hanging all the quilts out to air. Grandma and Pappy stayed in our room, and Jeanie and I slept in the alcove next to the dining room. We didn't mind. There was only a curtain covering it and we could hear them talk; we listened until our eyes got too tired to hear anymore and closed.

There was lots of work to be done. Jeanie and I had carefully brought the china up from the basement yesterday. It still needed to be washed, the silver polished and the house cleaned and dusted. Then I remembered the best part about getting ready for Christmas was the baking. My grandmother always made the pies when she got here and for a minute, I was lost in the taste of lemon meringue, berry, pumpkin, apple, and mincemeat. Mom and Dad made batches of cookies ahead of time. Our favorites were the chocolate but they also made peanut butter, oatmeal and refrigerator cookies, plus cakes. Last weekend my aunt and uncle came to help make our traditional Christmas oyster candy: Sea foam, formed into a small ball, then dipped in chocolate and rolled in crushed Spanish peanuts or walnuts.

"Do you want to go down the hill again?"

Jeanie's question brought a swift answer, "No, I'm hungry. Let's go home."

Food was forgotten when we saw the front yard was covered with new snow and not a mark on it. We looked at each other, "Snow angels!"

"C'mon," I yelled, "let's make some for Grandma and Pappy."

Jeanie ran next to me. "Yeah, and some snow people too!"

When there were wide tracks in the snow from rolling snow figures, and we were surrounded by snow angels, Jeanie and I stood up and ran towards another large area, "Hurry, we have lots more to go and we still haven't done all the snow family yet."

Jeanie dragged behind, "I wish our yard wasn't so big."

"It's a surprise for Grandma and Pappy. They'll be here next week."

We laid down in the snow again, spread out our arms and legs and moved them sideways.

"Hey girls, come on in. It's lunch time."

Jeanie and I brushed the white flakes off our clothes and stamped our boots. Mom opened the door for us, "You're both soaked to the skin. Go in the bathroom, and take off those wet clothes. I'll hang them up to dry after I get your warm pajamas."

"Mom, how long will that take? We only made two snow people and we have a lot more. It's not finished." Jeanie nodded as I spoke.

"Well, have some tomato soup and a cheese sandwich. I'll see if I can find your old snow suits—hopefully, they'll still fit."

My stomach was warmed by the soup as I got into my old suit. It was a little short but the heavy socks and boots covered me. Jeanie's looked fine because she tucked everything into the tops of her boots.

When she was dressed, I opened the front door and screamed. Three boys from the next street were knocking over our snow figures and scattering our angels. Mom came running to see what was wrong. I'm pretty fast but Mom beat me out the door. They ran away as soon as they saw her. She stopped long enough to put on her coat and boots, and marched right over to see their mother. I don't know what they talked about. When Mom got home, she just said, "The boys will help you rebuild them and all the snow people."

Sure enough, the next morning Jeanie and I watched Jackie and his two younger brothers build the snow people. They didn't speak to us, although every once in a while, they'd give us a dirty look.

"They don't look very happy."

"Nope," said Jeanie and then added, "they're sure building them bigger than we did."

Mom came out with hot chocolate and cookies for all five of us. "It's coming along fine, boys, thanks for the help." The dirty looks lightened a little.

"There's nothing for us to do," I told her, "they won't let girls help."

"Well, it's the season of peace on earth and it's also the birthday of the baby Jesus. Maybe you could build a crib for Him and a shelter for Mary and Joseph."

When Mom took the cups into the house, Jeanie and I put on heavy mittens. We each made a snow ball and packed it until it was hard as ice. Then we rolled it in the snow, stopping to pat it tighter as we went along. Jeanie made the largest one for the bottom. Mine was in the middle and the smallest would go on top. It was late afternoon and we weren't finished yet. When the boys trudged toward home, Frank, the youngest waved, "See you tomorrow."

Jeanie nodded, "Uh huh."

Jackie, the oldest, was quiet the next day. Jeanie and I finished before noon. I was concerned because the baby Jesus was lying on the ground. "Mom do you have any baby clothes for Jesus?"

She shook her head, "I only have pink."

Jackie spoke for the first time, "My mom probably has some from my younger brothers. I'll ask her."

For the first time, I really liked him. He turned to me, "Is it okay if we make snow people for our family too?"

I wanted to say no so bad because this was our surprise for Grandma and Pappy. I looked at the yard, "Jackie, there's not enough snow left."

His head drooped a little. It was Jimmy who came up with the solution. "There's plenty of snow in our yard. We could roll the figures there and haul 'em here on the toboggan."

Jackie brightened, "Yeah. Okay if we do that?"

I looked at Jeanie. She was nodding.

"Yeah, Jackie, it's okay. You guys made most of the snow people anyway." They ran across the lawn and were gone in a few seconds. There wasn't much snow left to slow them down.

My legs felt heavy and I wanted to cry. I wasn't sure how I'd explain to Grandma and Pappy.

Mom opened the door as we came up the steps, "Mom, we couldn't say no. They worked so hard. Now our surprise for Grandma and Pappy will be ruined."

Mom closed the door, "Come, sit with me on the couch." Jeanie and I sat on each side of her. "Your grandparents will be so proud of you two. That was a wonderful thing you did. Jackie and his brothers don't have grandparents. Eileen said both her folks and Tom's died years ago."

I was horrified. "No grandparents?" Jeanie had tears in her eyes.

Mom gave us a hug, "I'm glad you're letting them share in the fun."

After a few minutes she told us, "Your uncle will be here tomorrow and he's bringing some bales of straw for the manger and for people to sit on."

Jeanie and I got up and danced around. It was going to be a beautiful surprise.

Later that night, my last thought was sad, "No grandparents!"

It was barely light the next morning when we went outside after breakfast. Already, there were two new figures and the boys weren't in sight. Best of all, there was a blue cap on Baby Jesus' head and a small blue baby blanket covering Him. Mom gave us blue material for Mary and a striped sheet for Joseph.

She also gave us an old apron for Grandma's snow figure and another for her own. I held hers to my face before I put it on. It smelled like cookies! We put my dad's old work shirt on his snow figure. Frances, our baby sister, got discarded rattles and a pink hat. Jeanie and I had a scarf around the necks of our figures and we put ice skates in front of them. We didn't use the skates a lot. Our ankles were so weak, most of the time they were almost dragging on the ice.

Pappy's figure was the only one not decorated.

Jeanie and I raced to the house, "Mom, what can we put on Pappy's snowman?"

"How about the scarf he left here last time."

We were searching the closet when the phone rang and Mom yelled, "Barbie, get that. My hands are full of flour."

It was my best friend, Katie. She lived next to Jackie and his family. "What's going on?"

I told her everything that happened. She was impressed.

"Hey, can Nancy and I come over and make snow people for our family too?" This was definitely getting out of hand. I sighed. They were our closest friends. Katie was my age and her sister, Nancy, was a year younger than Jeanie. We did a lot together.

"You'll have to roll them at your house. Our snow is almost gone."

Nancy came over and borrowed our toboggan, and once they started bringing over their snow figures, all our other friends wanted to do it too. For three days our yard was the busiest place in the neighborhood. It was pretty organized because Jackie showed them where to put their snow families.

We put the scarf around Pappy's neck, then finished decorating all our snow family faces. Everyone dressed their figures and no two were alike. Some were really funny. My favorite had a black top hat and a cane. Jeanie and I added a red ball for the nose, two coal eyes, and a mouth made of maraschino cherries. We managed to get four before my mom came in and said that was enough.

We only got in trouble one other time.

"Do you girls have my spatula out there?"

Jeanie dug it out of the snow and ran to the porch, "Here Mom. We needed to flatten the tops and bottoms of the snow people so they'd stack easier."

Mom surveyed the yard, "It's really coming together." She looked at us. "Next time, ask. I have an old one you can use."

My uncle brought the hay, and he and Jackie placed two big bales in the manger and set the rest around the yard. Jeanie and I made a crib for the baby Jesus from some of the loose pieces and scattered the rest around Joseph and Mary.

When one of our neighbors built a little shelter over them, Mom brought out a gold star from the Christmas decorations and put it on the small, sloped roof. It was beautiful. Jeanie and I could hardly wait until Grandma and Pappy got there.

"Mom do you think it'll last until Christmas?"

"I don't know, Barbie. It's supposed to snow."

"Oh noooo."

Happily, it didn't.

The next afternoon, Jeanie and I were in our parents' bedroom staring out the window.

"No sign of them." Jeanie cast an anxious look at Mom.

"Don't worry. It's early yet. Do you girls want some lunch?"

We shook our heads. Our eyes never left the driveway.

Finally, Pappy's car pulled in.

They were barely out of the car when we flew into their arms.

It was several minutes before Grandma finally looked up and saw the yard. "What's all this?"

"It's your Christmas present." I pointed to the family near Joseph, Mary and the baby Jesus, "That's you and Pappy and Mom, Dad, Frances, Jeanie and me."

"And some of the neighbors made snow families too," Jeanie added.

Pappy stared at the decorated yard, "This is amazing."

They loved their snow people. Grandma added a scarf to hers and Pappy put one of his caps on his. Now, it looked just like him.

Later, Jackie's mother came to see Mom. "Thank you so much for this."

"Eileen, the kids did all the work."

Eileen looked at all the activity; there was lots of shouting and laughing. She shook her head and smiled, "It's been a long time since I've seen them so excited about something."

A lot of people were excited about it. They walked by and stopped to talk. My dad brought out some old folding chairs and put them on the sidewalk near the porch.

"Dave, it's too cold to sit outside."

"Just wait and see." was all he said.

For the next few days, in between making pies, my grandmother was outside several times a day talking with the neighbors. One afternoon Pappy and some of the other men who were gathered around his old Ford, decided to join in the fun and started building a huge snowman and a Santa Claus.

We helped for a while but they seemed to want to do it themselves, so a bunch of us went to Packard Hill. Some of the kids didn't have sleds so we took cardboard boxes.

Going down the hill on a piece of cardboard is wild. Not only does it smooth out the snow and make it slicker, there's no steering. Sometimes we spun around and around, finally spilling out into the snow. Once I went down backwards. At the bottom, Jeanie was cracking up.

"You yelled, 'Ahhhhhhh' all the way down."

"I was trying to turn around," I said with dignity.

It didn't stop her laughter. "You were wiggling and jumping all over the place," she said in between gasps for breath.

We grabbed our cardboards and climbed back to the top. This time I sat in the middle and held each side tightly. It worked; I went to the bottom sitting forward.

"That was better," Jeanie said.

"And boring."

"Really?"

I nodded, "Definitely."

Back to the top of the hill.

Jeanie went backwards with me this time and screamed all the way. It was great fun.

By the time we got home, the snowman and Santa Claus were done. They were way bigger than the other snow figures. We opened the back door—the house smelled yummy. Grandma looked up, "Oh there you are. Good, the bread is done. We're going to eat in a few minutes." She started singing, "'Up on the housetop, click, click, click...'" Then she winked. "Santa comes tomorrow night, don't forget."

No chance of that. It was all we thought about.

Christmas Eve was a long day. Lots of the neighbors brought visitors to see the snow families. Another aunt and uncle and two cousins came over with gifts, and Mom brought out presents for them.

Finally, it was supper time. After we ate, Jeanie and I put out a plate of cookies and a glass of milk for Santa and went to bed. I think I heard the door shut when Mom and Grandma left for Midnight mass. I thought I was too excited to sleep, but I didn't hear them come back.

Jeanie and I were up before dawn. We stood over the heat registers and quietly dressed. We didn't dare wake Mom and Dad yet.

Jeanie peeked down the hall and whispered, "I think they might be up, there are lights in the living room."

We looked through the crack in the door. The Christmas tree was lit and there were presents. Lots of them.

Jeanie spoke first, "Wow!"

I couldn't say a word. Under the branches were two brand new *Flexible Flyers*, exactly alike. They looked so bright and shiny in the Christmas lights. Quietly we lifted them out so we could see them. They were longer than the ones we had. Now, with my legs straight, I could go down Packard even faster. I ran my fingers over the bright red runners. They looked skinnier and very fast.

We didn't hear my dad until he spoke, "Look underneath."

I turned my sled over. I had chosen the right one; it had my name painted on it. Jeanie's name was on her sled too.

My dad smiled, "Now you won't get them mixed up. I'll

put your old sleds away until Frances gets big enough."

When she came in with Pappy and Grandma, Frances wasn't interested in sleds. She ran to the doll and teddy bear as soon as she saw them, first picking up one, then the other, and finally holding one in each arm.

Mom was wiping her hands on a towel as she walked in. "Well, the turkey and dressing are in the oven. We should be able to eat about noon or so."

Everyone opened their presents. My grandparents agreed the snow people were the best Christmas gift of all. They gave us a lot of kisses and thanked us over and over. Pappy got his camera and fiddled with it. "I'll take everyone's picture in the yard this afternoon."

I was anxious to get on my new sled, "C'mon, Jeanie, let's go outside."

Mom put her foot down. "No! Not before you eat breakfast and it gets light."

It took *forever* for the sun to come up.

The cold lasted almost a week but the snow people came to an end three days after Christmas. Mom and Grandma were in the kitchen listening to the radio; I was reading my new Nancy Drew mystery and Jeanie was playing with the toy horses Santa brought her.

I snapped my book shut when I heard Mom shout, "Girls, get your snow suits on. Hurry! The radio said the storm tonight is going to be big with lots of snow. All the wash is still on the line."

Outside Mom was already pulling clothespins off as fast as she could. She handed us the pillow cases, all the kitchen towels and some clothes. "Take them inside and help your grandmother hang them in the basement. They're frozen stiff. I'll get the rest of these inside while you two clear everything out of the yard."

Jeanie and I put the chairs on the porch and piled the decorations on top. Most of the neighbors came to claim theirs, and my uncle picked up the hay bales. I removed Pappy's hat last.

The magic was gone. At dusk our snow families were just ghostly figures.

The next morning the yard was piled high with snow. The figures underneath were now mountains. One of the areas sloped down the sidewalk a long way. It looked like my wish for a sloping hill had come true.

"Think we could get our sleds up there?"

Jeanie punched a hole in the snow bank. Flakes flew everywhere. "Nah, too soft. Let's go to Packard. Probably the big kids have already iced it with cardboard."

Then her eyes sparkled, "I bet our new sleds will go all the way across."

I nodded. "I think it's time to find out."

And, yeah, it *was* a long walk back, but it was worth it.

Barbara Barrett is a published author and poet who loves and appreciates words. Her articles and poetry have appeared on blogs, websites and in fanzines. Her book, *Moon-Maze, a Collection of Poetry and Prose* won an NCPA award in 2020. *The Wordbook. An Index Guide to the Poetry of Robert E. Howard* (2009) and several of her essays have received awards from the Robert E. Howard Foundation.

"Tomboy Tales: The Christmas Surprise" is Barbara's fourth publication in an NCPA anthology. The short story "Harold's Search" appeared in *More Birds of a Feather* and her articles "Quality or Quantity" and "R and R" were published in *Destination: The World*, volumes 1 and 2.

She lives in Northern California and is a member of the NCPA, the Elk Grove Writers Group and the Elk Grove Writers Guild. She can be reached at barbara_barrett@sbcglobal.net.

A PERFECT JOURNEY

CHARLENE JOHNSON

Walking through the serene magnificence
Of a cold, winter forest,
After an early Thanksgiving dinner,
Keeping up the long-held tradition
Of finding a perfect Christmas tree,
In the footsteps of animals
Who are constant visitors,
Among pristine evergreen trees large and small,
Their pine branches newly covered with snow,
For me,
It's not about finding
A perfectly symmetrical tree
To fill with fancy ornaments
And lengths of colorful garland,
It is the perfect journey,
Shared with family
That will be remembered
And cherished
Throughout the years.

NCPA * OUR PURPOSE * WHO WE ARE * WHAT WE DO

Northern California Publishers & Authors (NCPA) is an alliance of independent publishers, authors, and publishing professionals in Northern California.

Formed in 1991 as Sacramento Publishers Association, then expanded to Sacramento Publishers and Authors and eventually to NCPA, our purpose is to foster, encourage, and educate authors, small publishers, and those interested in becoming authors and publishers.

We support small indie presses, self-publishers and aspiring authors at our monthly meetings by covering topics such as self- and traditional publishing, editing, book design, tax & legal issues, and marketing. Since the 2020 pandemic, monthly meetings have temporarily been moved to Zoom, but NCPA will resume in-person meetings, in addition to continuing Zoom meetings, after the quarantine is lifted.

Service providers who cater to the publishing industry – illustrators, cover designers, editors, etc. – are also invited to join NCPA as associate members.

In addition to our annual NCPA Book Anthology, for *members only*, which started again in 2019, NCPA holds an annual Book Awards Competition for both *members, and non- members.* The NCPA Book Awards Competition celebrated our 26th year with the entry of 37 books published in 2019.

NCPA also gives back to the community through proceeds from a Silent Auction during our Book Awards Banquets in the forms of: $1000 scholarship to a college-bound, local high school senior intending to pursue a publishing or writing-related degree; 916-Ink, which empowers youth through the published, written word; Mustard Seed School for underprivileged youth; and Friends of the Sacramento Public Library who provide books to the homes of underprivileged children.

Check out our website www.norcalpa.org for information on our next Book Awards Competition, the next anthology and information on how to join NCPA.

OTHER NCPA ANTHOLOGIES

Purchase anthologies at Amazon, Samati Press, or in person from any author in the Holiday Anthology. Anthologies are also available in eBook format. Information on each author in all anthologies can be found on the NCPA website: www.norcalpa.org.

BIRDS OF A FEATHER

An NCPA Anthology

A Collection of Short Stories about Animals

From their size, color, and the way they see the world, animals are diverse—and so are the delightful stories in this anthology. Ranging from legends and true tales of wildland bears to a memorable veterinary house call and stories of humans who become animals (or act like them), this collection is all about animals and our relationships with them. Meet rabbits, lizards, guinea pigs, potbelly pigs, horses, seals, owls, spiders, coyotes, wolves, elephants, and of course plenty of cats and dogs who will touch your heart and remind you that no matter how many legs we have, we all have much in common.

MORE BIRDS OF A FEATHER
An NCPA ANTHOLOGY
A Collection of Short Stories about Animals and Other Things

Within these pages are thirty non-fiction stories—some happy, some sad; some exciting, some glad; some daring, some caring— about a variety of animals. Add a little fiction: one far-out adventure and one fantasy, and toss in a couple of on-going series, previously introduced in *Birds of a Feather*.

There's Nacht, our resident feral cat who presents Tux, then our fun shape-shifters Dex and Felicity as the red fox and Arctic fox. Meet two elk and three penguins; a bunny that wouldn't give up; two elephants; a goat on the run; a potty-trained pig; two squirrels; and a bunch of wild birds, including a gosling, plus tame chickens: Lady Cluck and her girls; lizards in the Caribbean; crickets; a gorilla; a bear; a tortoise; and a variety of cats and dogs.

And a partridge in a pear tree? Maybe not, but the second NCPA anthology from 2019 is a lot of chirping fun.

Take a journey around the world with 35 authors from NCPA as they share their stories covering nearly every continent and a vast array of cultures. This collection of charming and endearing tales will take you on excursions beyond your own backyard from breathtaking trips of a lifetime to harrowing adventures and comical misadventures.

Enjoy more than thirty non-fiction stories, including: A Long-awaited Trip to Greece * "Wogging" in Ireland * China by Train * Ghosts in BC * and a First-Time Flight from Nigeria to America. If you're looking for fiction, discover the secret behind *Lance's Toboggan of Miracles,* follow the further adventures of Knacht, the Wanderer who stops wandering, and continue the fantasy adventures of our favorite shape-shifters, Dex and Felicity (introduced in NCPA's 2019 anthologies: *Birds of a Feather* and *More Birds of a Feather*), as they take their romance on the road with a honeymoon in Hawaii.

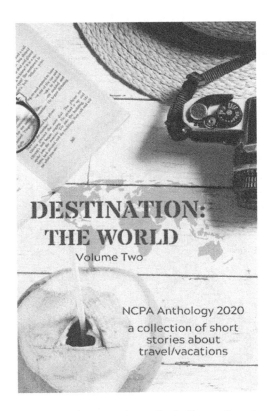

DESTINATION: THE WORLD
Volume Two

NCPA Anthology 2020
a collection of short stories about travel/vacations

Enjoy more than thirty stories, including: the Loma Prieta earthquake; a missing earring in Williamsburg, VA; a trip to Havana, Cuba; a mistaken identity in Italy; the Nigeria-Biafra Civil War; a search for weapons in Israel; and a near-arrest in Italy. Join a "sneaky boy" when he becomes a stowaway child aboard a ship migrating from Spain in 1907 and find how a sanctuary in Scotland led to the battlefield in NY in 1758. Immerse yourself in this diverse, one-of-a-kind NCPA Anthology.

In addition, this volume features the 4th fantasy installment of the red Fox and the Great Horned Owl, our favorite shape-shifters, Dex and Felicity as they meet the Menehune's in Hawaii, and the 4th installment of Nacht, the feral cat, and his adventures.

This *Destination: The World, Volume Two*, covers it all from A to Z: America to Zimbabwe, and everywhere in-between. There's a story within these pages for everyone.

Made in the USA
Monee, IL
15 February 2021